T0286953

Cambridge Elements ≡

Elements in Environmental Humanities
edited by
Louise Westling
University of Oregon
Serenella Iovino
University of North Carolina at Chapel Hill
Timo Maran
University of Tartu

ANTHROPOSCREENS

Mediating the Climate Unconscious

Julia Leyda
Norwegian University of Science and Technology

CAMBRIDGE
UNIVERSITY PRESS

Shaftesbury Road, Cambridge CB2 8EA, United Kingdom

One Liberty Plaza, 20th Floor, New York, NY 10006, USA

477 Williamstown Road, Port Melbourne, VIC 3207, Australia

314–321, 3rd Floor, Plot 3, Splendor Forum, Jasola District Centre, New Delhi – 110025, India

103 Penang Road, #05–06/07, Visioncrest Commercial, Singapore 238467

Cambridge University Press is part of Cambridge University Press & Assessment, a department of the University of Cambridge.

We share the University's mission to contribute to society through the pursuit of education, learning and research at the highest international levels of excellence.

www.cambridge.org
Information on this title: www.cambridge.org/9781009317672
DOI: 10.1017/9781009317702

First published 2023

A catalogue record for this publication is available from the British Library.

ISBN 978-1-009-31767-2 Paperback
ISSN 2632-3125 (online)
ISSN 2632-3117 (print)

Anthroposcreens

Mediating the Climate Unconscious

Elements in Environmental Humanities

DOI: 10.1017/9781009317702
First published online: July 2023

Julia Leyda
Norwegian University of Science and Technology
Author for correspondence: Julia Leyda, julia.leyda@ntnu.no

Abstract: *Anthroposcreens* frames the "climate unconscious" as a reading strategy for film and television productions during the Anthropocene. Drawing attention to the affects of climate change and the broader environmental damage of the Anthropocene, this Element mobilizes its frame in concert with other tools from cultural and film studies – such as debates over Black representation – to provide readings of the underlying environmental themes in Black American and Norwegian screen texts. These bodies of work provide a useful counterpoint to the dominance of White Anglo-American stories in cli-fi while also ranging beyond the boundaries of the cli-fi genre to show how the climate-unconscious lens functions in a broader set of texts. Working across film studies, cultural studies, Black studies, and the environmental humanities, *Anthroposcreens* establishes a cross-disciplinary reading strategy of the "climate unconscious" for contemporary film and television productions. This title is also available as Open Access on Cambridge Core.

Keywords: Norwegian film and television, race and environmental humanities, environmental humanities and film and television studies, climate fiction, petroculture

ISBNs: 9781009317672 (PB), 9781009317702 (OC)
ISSNs: 2632-3125 (online), 2632-3117 (print)

Contents

1 Introduction

Anthroposcreens: Mediating the Climate Unconscious grows out of two of the most compelling quandaries I have faced in the past decade as the concept of the Anthropocene has taken hold in humanities scholarship. First: my frustration that mainstream screen climate fiction (cli-fi) so often repeats Hollywood conventions that dramatize the survival of White patriarchal reproductive futurism embodied by the nuclear family. Surely, White Americans cannot be the only people in the United States affected by climate crisis, toxicity, or extreme weather; indeed, decades of research into the environmental justice movement amply document the uneven distribution of such "slow violence" within the United States and globally (Nixon 2011). Then why have my screen cli-fi seminars been stuck watching Dennis Quaid rescuing his "son" Jake Gyllenhaal, and Michael Shannon obsessing over protecting his family, semester after semester? How can cli-fi scholarship resist reinscribing the mostly-White-male film canon and thus reproducing that imbalance?[1]

A second quandary motivating this project is the bafflement I felt upon realizing that Norway, Europe's biggest petroleum producer, had no domestic *oeuvre* of fiction films or television series about that industry until 2015. Where was their *Dallas* (1987–91), their *Giant* (1956)? Unlike that of the United States, Norwegian screen culture has ignored oil for the almost-half-century since its discovery. Interrogating that long silence has led me to theorize a specifically Norwegian screen petroculture, inspired by North America–based scholarship but tailored to its own, quite different context.

After pursuing these two provocative research questions separately, I recognized a third challenge: to bring them together to productively speak to one another, in part as a test case for the reading strategy foregrounding the climate unconscious. With its dual focus on contemporary Black American and Norwegian films and television series, *Anthroposcreens* addresses the problematic predominance of Whiteness in US screen cli-fi by analyzing how Black film and television address climate issues (however obliquely), and how Norwegian screen texts negotiate the absences and presences of both oil and race. In doing so, this study engages academic approaches and concepts often siloed within different segments of film and television studies or in disciplines such as Black

---

[1] Following the police murder of George Floyd in May 2020, most US-based style guides adopted a policy of capitalizing "Black," with less consensus on "White." I follow the reasoning of Nell Irvin Painter (2020) and Kwame Anthony Appiah (2020) in their commentaries published that summer: Whiteness and Blackness are both socially constructed identities and thus both merit a capital letter. Further, Painter argues that the capital "W" serves "to situate 'Whiteness' within the American ideology of race, within which 'Black,' but not 'White,' has been hypervisible as a group identity" (n.p.). In quoted material, I remain faithful to the original.

studies or Scandinavian studies. Juxtaposing these two sets of case studies presses key concepts from these areas into engagement with one another and with concepts in environmental humanities; in a way, somewhat incongruously. Could *Anthroposcreens* have chosen to interrogate another non-Anglophone national screen context instead of Norwegian? Of course. But the point is not to argue for the exceptionality of Norway here; on the contrary, for this intervention to yield a truly versatile reading strategy, it needs to extend in myriad directions and develop its approaches with a flexibility that can adapt to a range of contexts. After years of working as a scholar within Anglophone, American studies circles, moving to Norway has stretched the boundaries of my corpus; I hope that future research in this direction will take up screen texts in other languages and national contexts. As an English-speaking scholar, with reading knowledge of Norwegian and German, I also acknowledge my own limitations. Presenting work to more experienced colleagues, I struggle against self-accusations of dilettantism for diving into Scandinavian studies relatively recently; indeed, there is only so much one scholar can knowledgeably cover, which is why research is properly seen as a collective effort.

Crossing disciplines can be exciting and frightening, and it brings its own uncertainties and innovations. As Mieke Bal argues in her essential guide to interdisciplinary cultural analysis, concepts can do "the methodological work that disciplinary traditions used to do," but only if "they are kept under scrutiny through a confrontation with, not application to, the cultural objects being examined" (2002: 24). To do this work, concepts must travel, as Bal elaborates, "between disciplines, between individual scholars, between historical periods, and between geographically dispersed academic communities." *Anthroposcreens* brings into conversation, and at times confrontation, concepts and objects of study that are not ordinarily put together, in the hope that readers will experience a new sense of something clicking into place. In its selection of primary texts and secondary sources, *Anthroposcreens* stakes out new ground, calibrating its position relative to a constellation of fields, many of which have often centered around mainstream Anglo-American cultural and academic production at the expense of any consideration of (differently positioned) margins, a tendency that reproduces the messy universalizing inherent in some theorizations of the Anthropocene.

The geological periodization of the Anthropocene has sparked debates about its starting points, its scientific definition, and its travels across disciplines; however, these are not the central focus here. Suffice it to say that the Anthropocene refers to the relatively recent, measurable imprint of human activity on the systems of the Earth. Through the increasing consumption of fossil fuels among other practices, people in developed countries (some more than others) have altered Earth systems that were formerly seen as "natural," such that even disasters like hurricanes and earthquakes may now be described as (at least partially) anthropogenic.[2] As Eva Horn and Hannes Bergthaller point out, humans have crossed a threshold whereby "[o]ur present is the future that the environmental movement has been warning us against." The Anthropocene is the "now" time for readers of this study; whether the era began with European colonialism or the Industrial Revolution(s) or the detonation of atomic bombs is not my main topic here (Horn and Bergthaller 2020: 2, 25–30). More than just a name for our era, the Anthropocene concerns the humanities because, according to literary scholar Elizabeth DeLoughrey, "the Anthropocene is *material* in that it concerns what can be measured and experienced, and it is *representational* in that it raises vital questions as to how the planet as a system can be signified" (2019: 3) My usage functions alongside media scholar Joanna Zylinska's observation that "the Anthropocene has become a new epistemological filter through which we humans can see ourselves" (2018: 3). The Anthropocene – era and concept – constitutes an unavoidable substrate for contemporary popular culture, and like the term cli-fi, has been much debated and reviled. Yet, like cli-fi, the currency of the usage "Anthropocene" is evidence that new problematics and critical foci often demand (even clunky and problematic) new categories.

Today's (and tomorrow's) environmental crises are not going away. Indeed, they increasingly dominate all varieties of media. *Anthroposcreens* examines both critically acclaimed and widely enjoyed films and series because together they provide a way to understand how media address (or avoid) environmental issues and attitudes of mass audiences. I have more to say on this than can fit into this short form, and there will be more to come. More importantly, I encourage more scholars to collaborate across disciplines and to reshape methodological and citational practices. This collective endeavor feels urgent because, to paraphrase Donna Haraway, the crisis is so dire that we should be throwing everything we have at it, in the hope that something might work. I propose to throw more popular culture studies at the problem, because reading for what I term the *climate unconscious* can open up more quotidian "entertainment" screen texts to critical climate awareness, and because we don't have time to wait.

---

[2] I have little interest in scoring points for or against a particular term or concept like the Anthropocene, the Capitalocene, the Plantationocene, Wasteocene, and so forth, nor should my title's pun on the most widely used term be read as an assertion that the Anthropocene concept is unproblematic. Indeed, I concur with critiques of its multiple erasures, and with Steven Mentz (2019) that the academic fixation on the Anthropocene concept amounts to a "Neologismcene" in which the new terms themselves create space for creative new ways of thinking, which are needed now more than ever.

1.1 Reading the Climate Unconscious

Anthroposcreens demonstrates how contemporary movies and television series, regardless of theme or genre, can be productively read through the climate unconscious. Much of my recent work examines how popular screen texts channel existing tropes and affects in ways that obliquely mediate contemporary climate anxieties. For example, if you asked the average person what the long-running series *The Walking Dead* (2010–22) is about, the vast majority would say a zombie apocalypse, not climate change. Yet the series was filmed largely in the Deep South during summer, and the actors often appear soaked in sweat due to the subtropical weather conditions of that region. However, reading this postapocalyptic drama with the climate unconscious in mind, I developed the concept of a future "post–air conditioning era" to discuss the aesthetic and affective properties of on-screen sweat as more than just a problem for makeup artists and costumers. Consuming shows set in the near future in which characters perspire profusely allows viewers accustomed to the banal comforts of air conditioning to contextualize depictions of extreme heat and its material and affective consequences within their already-existing cultural awareness about increasingly inhospitable weather (Leyda 2016b; Leyda 2021). Resolutely focusing on both pro-filmic and media production dimensions, I argue that reading the climate unconscious affords a fresh take on contemporary popular screen culture as premediations of the affects and embodiments of a possible post–air conditioning future.

Anthroposcreens posits just such an approach to excavate the structures of feeling that characterize current film and television's particular ways of processing environmental thinking. In the current era of convergent transmedia, with the global spread of digital distribution platforms for screen entertainment moving in parallel with global activist movements such as (social media–fueled) youth climate strikes, I identify and analyze the ways environmental issues find expression aesthetically and affectively in clusters of media texts. This study theorizes how public discourses around environmental issues, even when not foregrounded, contribute to a baseline awareness that producers and consumers of screen texts cannot help but participate in, however intuitively (Leyda 2021: 101). Indeed, the further into the background the climate unconscious seems to recede, the more crucial it is to examine it.

Notably, many scholars in the environmental humanities have developed similar concepts that examine theme, setting, and/or subtexts in cultural productions: Lawrence Buell's "environmental unconscious" (2009), Patricia Yaeger's "energy unconscious" (2011), Roman Bartosch's "petroleum unconscious" (2019), Harry Pitt Scott's "energopolitical unconscious" (Scott 2020), and Mark Bould's "Anthropocene unconscious" (2021). The popularity of these "unconsciouses" across academic generations testifies to the concept's effectiveness at doing critical work, and *Anthroposcreens* aims to harness this tradition in its study of contemporary screen media. I coin my own as an acknowledgment of these related terms – which have proven generative – with different lenses attending to various environmental thematics. Yet my contribution, the climate unconscious, brings to the conversation a specific focus on the at-times unwieldy and diffuse topic of climate crisis. More than any other aspect of the Anthropocene, a widespread awareness of climate change worms its way into every form of media, to the extent that contact with media means it cannot be avoided. As Adrian Ivakhiv argues in his foray into "a Jamesonian ecocriticism": "the contemporary world system can hardly be thought today without reference to the larger – and until recently unthinkable – totality of the ecological system which both sustains and interpenetrates with the political-economic system" (2008: 99). I argue here for a similar analytical standpoint, underscoring the way an understanding of climate change in particular undergirds contemporary audiences' frames of reference for their (our) understandings of screen texts. While the other "unconsciouses" I have mentioned operate along similar lines and offer inspiring frameworks for further teaching and research, my method takes as a starting point the fact that climate crisis is the single issue that, in a way, stands for popular understandings of the Anthropocene. Enabling a clearer awareness of this fact means reading those texts for the climate unconscious, and thereby building a critical reading method for recognizing screen media's myriad premediations of human climate futures and for unpacking aesthetic and affective responses to them.

1.2 Structures of Feeling, the Unconscious, and Affect

In the conceptual work here, my archive is eclectic, incorporating recent scholarship but also often reaching back to theorists whose work may no longer grace today's cutting-edge bibliographies. Yet as Sara Ahmed argues about feminist citational practice, a past work that has laid out important "desire lines, created by not following the official paths laid out by disciplines" can still function as a "companion text ... whose company enabled you to proceed on a path less trodden" (2017: 15–16). *Anthroposcreens* builds its methodology out of a set of questions and concepts that took shape under the loose umbrella of cultural studies, forged at the Birmingham Center under Raymond Williams and Stuart Hall in the United Kingdom and taken up by humanities and social science scholars around the world. The central premise of the cultural studies approach is that the popular culture of any given period has much to tell about the time in which it is produced: its politics, its society, its anxieties. The climate unconscious takes its place among the constellation of companion "unconsciouses" from cultural studies and environmental humanities I have described, all indebted to Fredric Jameson, who himself adapted Raymond Williams's paradigm of "structures of feeling" and took it in a new direction, framing narrative as "a socially symbolic act," as the subtitle of his 1981 book *The Political Unconscious* explains. That book's central concept brings into conversation the structures of the unconscious, drawn from psychoanalytic theory à la Freud via Lacan, with Marxist models of ideology, spawning generations of updates, critiques, and riffs. Equally crucial to this study's theoretical work is Williams's notion of "structures of feeling," which I see as a precursor concept to the collective connotations in recent usages of "affect" in exemplary scholarship by Steven Shaviro (2016) and Nicole Seymour (2018), for example.

Structure of feeling points to the fact that affects, emotions, and feelings are not exclusively individualized, but also complexly connected to the social and historical world. Hall explains that Williams saw this structure as embedded and taken for granted in a specific time and place, signifying

> what it is like to think and act about a particular problem in a society. It seems to come naturally to people who are inside the society because they share the results of the historical experience which has produced this particular set of ideas about the family, culture, masculinity, the economy, et cetera. It is these structures of feeling that are reflected or expressed in the different social practices. (Hall 2016: 37)

This term indicates the sets of shared sensibilities and values specific to a located moment, often articulated through artistic forms and conventions, including mediated forms of entertainment. The connection to textual expression, including film and television as social practice, as well as its relation to the collective, marks my understanding of structures of feeling (Turner 2006). Although in this short Element I restrict my corpus to screen texts, I also discern the climate unconscious in other forms of cultural expression such as literary and genre fiction, comics, and video games, for example.

As it thinks with and builds upon other articulations of a variety of "unconsciouses," *Anthroposcreens* is not the first study to consider emotions in connection with contemporary environmental crisis, and it contributes to a growing set of studies of eco-affect. Important investigations of cinema and the environment over the past two decades have marked out important territory in the shared interdisciplinary spaces of film studies and environmental humanities (Cubitt 2005; Willoquet-Maricondi 2010; Pick and Narraway 2013; Weik von Mossner 2014). Several studies interested in the environment underscore emotional engagement, building a crucial critical vocabulary for the emerging field. The term "solastalgia" was coined by environmental philosopher Glenn Albrecht et al. (2007) to describe the grief of watching the destruction or transformation of one's home, as a result of environmental damage, for example. Related film studies frameworks, such as E. Ann Kaplan's "pre-trauma" (2016) and Anil Narine's "eco-trauma" (2014), draw on trauma studies to describe and understand how screen media portray the pain and psychological damage that many experience when facing the lived effects of climate crisis firsthand. In the energy humanities, Stephanie LeMenager's concept of "petromelancholia" (2014) aptly expresses the emotional experience of loss that many in the developed world (will) feel as access to cheap energy declines and taken-for-granted conveniences recede.

Beyond academia, the notion of climate anxiety has taken hold in popular media and mental health circles, causing concern about young people in particular (Wu, Snell, and Samji 2020), a group who take center stage in Section 2. Climate anxiety afflicts even (or especially) the children of wealthy White Americans, as in a storyline during Season 2 of the HBO drama *Big Little Lies* (2017–19), when a protagonist's daughter is found hiding in the second-grade classroom closet, and a subsequent therapy session uncovers severe anxiety fueled by schoolwork about the environmental crises threatening Earth's future. The emotional burden on today's "climate generation," as environmental studies scholar Sarah Jaquette Ray avers, makes it difficult to find "the energy and desire to engage with, not turn away from, the crises we face" (2020: 9). Yet, Ray continues, facing the crises of the Anthropocene means facing fear and anxiety: "As climate change becomes felt by more people, the boundary between those who worry about a future apocalypse and those who are experiencing that apocalypse right now will further blur." Such worries do not exist in a vacuum, however; they intersect with other anxieties that fuel myriad social ills.

Indeed, climate anxiety may be bundled together with xenophobia, sexism, and White supremacist thinking: "Racism is not an accidental byproduct of environmentalism; it has been a constant reference point . . . . Intense emotions mobilize people, but not always for the good of all life on this planet" (Ray 2021: n.p.). Given the complex imbrications of feelings and politics that surround the issue of climate change, intersectional feminist inquiry is a crucial method in the toolbox for recognizing and unpacking the climate unconscious. An era coterminous with renewed social and political upheavals around race, class, gender, and colonialism, the Anthropocene demands con-textualization within these ongoing power struggles. The central premise ani-mating the environmental humanities, according to Serpil Oppermann and

Serenella Iovino, "is that the urgent environmental problems that stretch from the geological to the biological are also essentially social and cultural issues deeply interwoven with economic and political agendas" (2017: 3). Zylinska speculates that "the very emergence of the Anthropocene as a proposition and discourse has acted as fodder for White supremacist tendencies by way of containing and perhaps temporarily warding off anxieties about the extinction of the White Man" (2018: 33; see also Daggett 2018; Malm and Zetkin Collective 2021). Rather than analyzing how screen texts represent and provoke feelings about the climate crisis and other environmental problems as if these problems existed in a vacuum, I take a broader approach, which I find yields more illuminating results; after all, environmental crisis doesn't exist neatly divided from problems related to inequality, nor is the reverse true.

1.3 Mediating the Climate Unconscious

Anthroposcreens picks out common threads running through its case studies to theorize how Anthropocene affects permeate contemporary screen texts as mediations of the climate unconscious. Its examples include television and film genres such as speculative and science fiction, thrillers, melodramas, and historical dramas, shining a light on Black US American and Norwegian productions frequently overlooked in ecomedia studies. Reaching outside the predominantly White Anglo-American canon of environmental films and television that have been loosely labeled cli-fi in the existing research, I have selected lesser-known or unexpected popular examples that yield fresh analyses and decenter the usual objects of environmental film and television studies.[3]

As part of this decentering impulse, *Anthroposcreens* offers permutations of the billion Black Anthropocenes that geologist Kathryn Yusoff (2018) insists upon, and thereby honors her exhortation to position Blackness and the ongoing trauma of colonialism at the heart of eco-critique. Moreover, this project brings her argument about racial politics in geology and environmental history into conversation with the racial politics of television and film studies. As Stuart Hall asserts about the practice of cultural studies analysis, "it has to be about politics, not just as a 'celebration' of the popular: it needs to be a way of investigating politics through culture" (Hall qtd. in Morley 2019: 10). In what follows, I create a theoretical framework for reading in conjunction aesthetics, affects, and politics as a way of thinking through race alongside environmental issues embedded in the climate unconscious. Taking up Black American film

---

[3] These are not the only categories that should be examined; in the scope of this abbreviated Element, there isn't space to consider additional national contexts or racialized groups, but the theoretical framework here could prove useful in constructing future research projects that can do so.

and television alongside the Norwegian also generates a productive friction to disrupt the assumption that Black screen texts are always "about" authentic realities of Blackness. Michael Boyce Gillespie underscores this problematic tendency in his rejection of "fidelity considerations of black film," asking instead, "What if black film is art and not the visual transcription of the black lifeworld?" (Gillespie 2016: 2, 157). This Element employs examples from disparate cultural contexts in part to contest that reductive assumption; not only must considerations of Anthropocene media include Black film and television, but they must also avoid isolating Black texts in a silo "about" Blackness and racism.

Just as screen Blackness can be over-racialized, screen Whiteness is often not racialized enough, particularly outside Anglophone contexts. Pairing Black US American film and television with Norwegian texts, *Anthroposcreens* calls for more attention to Whiteness across the Nordic *oeuvre*, in which race is rarely mentioned and Whiteness predominant but unmarked. In the majority-White Nordic countries, "the politics of race blindness and the discourse of Nordic exceptionalism delimit public discussions on racism" (Rastas 2019: 358). Yet, as film scholar Richard Dyer establishes, in cultural productions, "Whiteness is … always already predicated on racial difference, interaction, and domination, but that is true of all texts, not just those that take such matters as their explicit subject matter" (1997: 13). In recent years, "whiteness in the Nordic countries is in flux due to influxes of non-white migrants and the increased mobility and mobilization of domestic minorities like the Sámi, Jews, and Roma" (Lundström and Teitelbaum 2017: 151). Reading Norwegian popular media, then, *Anthroposcreens* foregrounds Whiteness's paradoxes as a way to ameliorate the current imbalance in which racialization is less frequently associated with White Norwegianness.

The structural logic of this Element follows its argument's logic. Section 2 reads for the climate unconscious in combination with Black cultural representation (on- and off-screen) to investigate the affective resonances and environmental politics of two Black US screen productions: *Queen Sugar* and *Black Panther*. The third section constitutes a bridge between Black and Norwegian contexts, unpacking the concept of "weather" in Black popular culture, interdisciplinary Black studies, and environmental humanities to foreground the ways that the Black US film *Fast Color* and the Norwegian series *Ragnarok* use weather (and the ability to change it) to spotlight youth, collectivity, and the operations of the climate unconscious in a new generation of cli-fi. Turning to the Norwegian series *Occupied* and *State of Happiness*, Section 4 interrogates the paradox in which, despite providing the economic basis of Norwegian prosperity, oil was rarely represented in that national screen culture until these recent, prestige productions, and even in these series climate change is either not mentioned or features only glancingly as a background theme.

In the ineffable process of scholarly accretion, my thinking throughout this project has led me to pose new questions building on the work of my academic forebears across the disciplines, crafting the theoretical frameworks required to work with my chosen texts. My citational practices, too, have grown out of my ongoing efforts to draw on scholars and fields whose work has been marginalized or ignored. As a White American emigrant academic, I thus forge ahead with my investigations of Black US and Norwegian screen productions, belonging to neither group but invested in rigorous humanities scholarship. Embedded in this framing is my acknowledgment of positionality and accountability, an awareness that "we" who perform this research are not vigilant enough about "our" assumptions and positionality; my corpus and my archive here take steps to mitigate that myopia. Mixing the methods of close reading case studies with delineating broader patterns within recent films and television series taken in cultural context, *Anthroposcreens* theorizes the importance of contemporary popular screen media in the elaboration and processing of environmental issues through their sometimes below-the-radar affective and aesthetic regimes.

2 Total Climate: Black Anthroposcreens

> Plotting within and against the plantation is a practice of cultivating life and kin that challenges the intertwined death-dealing logics of racism and ecocide.
>
> Janae Davis, Alex A. Moulton, Levi Van Sant, and Brian Williams[4]

> Afrofuturism allows the imagination not only to cure the injury but to imagine a world where the knife blade of colonialism escapes the Black body altogether.
>
> Tochi Onyebuchi[5]

What happens when Black artists create popular film and television in the Anthropocene? What does the climate unconscious as a reading strategy yield when focused on Black-created, Black-cast screen productions? As Kathryn Yusoff (2018) points out, an approach that overturns the structures and dynamics that brought about the Anthropocene requires a Black and Indigenous poetics at its center. This section, then, puts into practice that centering of Black creative power, to reveal, among other things, how Black cultural productions articulate a historically specific relation to Anthropocene legacies of extraction and enslavement. Even when Black films and television series participate in recognizably conventional entertainment genres such as family melodrama, superhero stories, and speculative fiction, the results are necessarily

---

[4] Davis et al. (2019, n.p.).   [5] Onyebuchi (2018, n.p.).

different in crucial ways. When Black creators guide the camera and narrate the stories, popular film and television often look and feel different, even when the genres are familiar, as theorists Simone Drake and Dwan Henderson remind us: "Black cultural producers respond to stakes of Black art that continue to be inextricably linked not only to the entertainment of white folk but also to the dependence of dominant culture upon static notions of Blacks as hypersexual, primitive (premodern), violent, lazy, feckless, conniving, childish, and ultimately lacking humanity" (2020: 10). The power of representation remains a crucial concern in the study of popular culture, as film scholar Nina Cartier explains: "Black audiences' engagement with Black characters on-screen is at once a matter of fantasy projection as well as the reification of a collective sense of self" (2014: 152). The sheer affective power of reframing popular genres to focus on Black characters and concerns cannot be underestimated, and that power is further amplified by the visibility of Black creative teams behind the camera; although investigations of Black popular culture have a rich archive, the contest over the politics of representation has not yet ended. For this reason, *Anthroposcreens* demonstrates that environmental humanities' inquiries into the operations of the climate unconscious in contemporary Black popular screen productions must be grounded in the vigorous ongoing debates about representation in Black film and media studies.

The decades-long critical conversation about Black representation continues to challenge and reinvigorate screen studies, in part because its fundamental questions are still relevant. The introduction to a 2014 dossier of articles on Black media notes that, thanks to the pathbreaking work of Stuart Hall in the 1980s and '90s, "issues of identity, representation, and politics will always converge around Blackness" (Smith-Shomade, Gates, and Petty 2014: 121). Three years later, Racquel Gates and Michael Boyce Gillespie wryly observe in their manifesto "Reclaiming Black Film and Media Studies," "[i]f the representation debate revival must occur, then at least reread Stuart Hall" (Ugwu 2019: 15). Hall's foundational 1992 essay "What Is This 'Black' in Black Popular Culture?" points out that Black popular culture is "bound to be contradictory," in part because the popular signifies both authenticity and commercialization; thus Black popular culture is "rooted in popular experience and available for expropriation at one and the same time" (108). In the twenty-first-century media landscape, Black artists have begun to achieve recognition, and screen-industry gatekeepers are slowly realizing that Black-centered movies and programs can win audience shares. Whether today's success stories will establish lasting industrial changes remains to be seen; securing not only creative roles but also gatekeeping positions such as executive and showrunner, as the successes of Oprah Winfrey, Ava DuVernay, Jordan Peele, and Tyler Perry demonstrate, may help this new flourishing avert the fate of the brief Black film boom in the 1990s (Ugwu 2019). Indeed, what Hall terms "the struggle over cultural hegemony" can never be decisively won, because "it is always about changing the dispositions and the configurations of cultural power, not getting out of it" (1993: 106–107). Breaking into and creating leadership positions and demanding greater creative control are two strategies that can contribute to shifting those configurations of racialized power in the industry.

Kristen Warner cautions against settling for "plastic representation," however, in which images "become hollowed, malleable signs with artificial origins," in pursuit of the sheen of diversity at the cost of depth or complexity (2017: 34). She aptly observes that

> [w]hen audiences, cultural critics, and even industry professionals buy into the subtle but popular belief that social progress occurs when the focus of representation is placed solely on the racially visible difference of above-and-below-the-line talent, it means that for industry gatekeepers and executives, less time has to be devoted to developing and appreciating the meaningful cultural and historical differences of those bodies. (36)

Warner's indispensable concept of "plastic representation" also carries environmental baggage, signaling the artificial, synthetic nature of box-ticking diversity ploys while connoting the malignancy of the substance itself, at least in the form of ocean plastic pollution, for example. And while today's Black screen productions increasingly feature Black talent behind the camera, including in writers' rooms and boardrooms, these films and television series still compete for popularity in a crowded global media market, and thus still often succeed with their forays into proven presold genres such as melodrama and speculative fiction.

This section develops an environmental humanities approach to particularities of the climate unconscious in two recent Black screen productions, *Queen Sugar* (2016–22) and *Black Panther* (2018). Both received critical acclaim for their commitment to representing Blackness on screen and showcasing Black talent throughout the cast, crew, and executive levels. While both are firmly rooted in popular genres, they also differ significantly: *Queen Sugar* is a woman-centered melodrama that revolves around family relationships, while the superhero blockbuster *Black Panther* caters to the Marvel Cinematic Universe's global fan base, even as it challenges them to embrace the first standalone Marvel film about a Black superhero. *Queen Sugar* is not widely available outside North America, perhaps owing to the longstanding feminization of the television melodrama and the myth that non-US audiences are not interested in Black stories, while *Black Panther* is an international box-office blockbuster that has streamed on two global portals (and even its smash global success purportedly came as a pleasant surprise to its parent company) (Wilkinson 2018). Here I employ these examples as a testing ground for an analysis weaving together environmental concerns that manifest in the climate unconscious and theoretical attention to Blackness in film and television studies, across genres, platforms, and degrees of popular success.

The disciplines of film and television studies and environmental humanities both continue to reckon with their own problematic histories of privileging Whiteness, and the pairing of *Queen Sugar* with *Black Panther* offers a rich opportunity to set key concepts from both areas into conversation with one another. As Gates and Gillespie lament, "the field of film studies was designed around the centering of heterosexual white men." Recognition of the inherent racism in the industry and in the scholarship has often led, as they point out, to superficial acts of additive inclusion and tokenism such as "the infamous 'race week' in any Intro film/media course" (Gates and Gillespie 2019: 13). Within environmental humanities, critical geographers call out formulations such as the color-blind conceptualization of the Plantationocene. Attempting to remedy the anthropocentrism of the Anthropocene and call attention to the plantation as a crucial site in its history, Donna Haraway's "Plantationocene" (2015) sets up, in the words of Davis et al., a "multispecies framing [that] minimizes the role of racial politics and leads to a flattened notion of 'making kin' that is inadequate for the creation of more just ecologies in the plantation present," which demands "ecological thought and action that is firmly rooted in struggles for justice." In their critique, Janae Davis et al. refer to Black plantation geographies by Katherine McKittrick and Clyde Woods that could have lent nuance and depth had Haraway consulted them (Davis et al. 2019: 3; 6–7). Arguing that a multispecies framing need not be a "multispecies flattening" that becomes color-blind in its formulations, which describe, for instance, plantation agriculture as "slavery of plants" (Davis et al. 2019: 5). Similarly, the task of decolonizing the discipline of film studies means examining that largely White academic discipline with new lenses, as Gates and Gillespie have argued. Bringing together methods and disciplinary frameworks from film and media studies with environmental humanities frequently means coming to terms with the blind spots enabled by histories of White academic privilege and finding ways to avoid the mistakes of even the most influential scholars.

Taking on board metadisciplinary critiques around Blackness and Whiteness within environmental humanities and film and media studies, I hope to highlight traces of what I term the "banal Anthropocene" in popular texts that are more frequently referenced in thematic relation to racial politics. In my discussion of *Queen Sugar* and *Black Panther*, I tease out some implications that will push beyond the (quite important and relevant) discussions about increasing Black representation on the screen and in the industry. By calling attention to subtexts of cultural knowledge, the climate-unconscious reading strategy encourages viewers to identify "premediations of possible climate-changed futures, a first step in facing those futures and imagining how it will feel to live in them" (Leyda 2021: 106). In these Black screen contexts, the climate unconscious can enhance understandings of the already complex layers of meaning accrued around local and global histories of White supremacy and oppression in settings such as rural Louisiana and the fictional Wakanda.

2.1 Reading the Cane Farm in *Queen Sugar*

Queen Sugar, a seven-season family drama on Oprah Winfrey's OWN network and created by award-winning filmmaker Ava DuVernay, has attracted attention as DuVernay's first television series and as one of a growing number of major-ity-Black-cast, auteur-driven "quality" television shows such as *Atlanta* (2016–), *Insecure* (2016–), *I May Destroy You* (2020), *Lovecraft Country* (2020), *Small Axe* (2020), and *Underground Railroad* (2021). Like most of these, *Queen Sugar* enjoys diverse creative teams, not only in terms of its producers, writers, cast, and music (by Meshell Ndegeocello), but also its all-female lineup of directors, including film directors like Julie Dash, Cheryl Dunye, Karyn Kusama, and Pratibha Parmar. The latter decision on the part of DuVernay "nearly tripled the number of first-time women directors of episodic television" for the year of 2016 (Williams 2019: 1044). The show's commitment to diversity shows in its roster of experienced talent. Ironically though, this risks playing into the limiting logic of auteur gatekeeping currently prevalent at major streaming platforms:

> When streamers do hire prominent people of color auteurs – take Shonda Rhimes or Barry Jenkins or even the Obamas for instance – the reality is that these creators often serve as the keepers of risk for the platform. Their presence signals diversity and innovation, but often leaves very little available to those other Black and Brown folks who might need the protection that accompanies experimentation. (Warner 2021)

However, airing on the flagship network of Winfrey's media empire, created by DuVernay, and distributed by her company, Array, the show possesses a more deep-rooted ethic of inclusion than PR-motivated "plastic representation." As I will discuss in relation to Viola Davis's company JuVee in the following section, Array positions itself in oppositional terms in its mission statement: "we are an independent film distribution and resource collective comprised of arts advocacy organizations, maverick volunteers, and rebel member donors worldwide. Our work is dedicated to the amplification of independent films by people of color and women filmmakers globally." The existence of Black-run media companies like JuVee, Harpo, and Array means that executives like Davis, Winfrey, and DuVernay have the leverage not only to support known talent among Black and women industry professionals, but also to mentor and elevate upcoming talent, such as debut director Cierra Glaude, who worked as a production assistant, director's assistant, and writer before helming three episodes of *Queen Sugar*'s fifth season (Fekadu 2021).

The series positions itself as a corrective in the realm of representation, featuring mostly Black characters, contexts, and stories as well as creators; moreover, its narrative and aesthetic form dovetails with those concerns, emphasizing the importance of loving support and collective struggle in a racist society. *Queen Sugar* interrogates the complex legacies of the Southern plantation, articulated through a contemporary Black Louisiana family's generations-long roots in a sugar-cane community. In this sense comparable to the blockbuster *Black Panther*, *Queen Sugar* takes scrupulous care in the intricacies and depths of its world-building: the *mise-en-scène* and cinematography are lush, even sumptuous, in their deployment of color, design, costuming, hairstyles, and landscape to construct the vibrant tone and vivid atmosphere of the story (see Figure 1). The series creates an air of authenticity in its Southern nostalgia for rural family homes, escaping cliché in part due to its departure from the usual Whiteness of such settings. At the start of the first season, the drama explicates the bonds and the tensions among three adult

Figure 1 Lush landscape shots of sugar-cane fields in *Queen Sugar* (2016–22) resonate with the histories of the Bordelons' enslaved ancestors and the enduring contemporary inequalities facing rural Black Americans

siblings as they revive their recently deceased father's faltering farm in southern Louisiana: the wealthy sister, Charley (Dawn Lyen-Gardner), relocates from Los Angeles, where she had managed her (now-estranged) basketball-star husband; the activist-journalist sister, Nova (Rutina Wesley), works in nearby New Orleans; and their younger brother Ralph Angel (Kofi Siriboe) has just been released from the penitentiary and takes over running the farm. *Queen Sugar*'s complex character arcs across seven seasons take up issues of abuse, addiction, gender, sexuality, class, health care, immigration, incarceration, folk tradition, respectability politics, ambition, and innumerable references to histories of slavery and the Black Atlantic and their enduring structures of racism in the present.

The main storyline in the series concerns the Bordelon siblings' struggle to re-establish their farm and start a community sugar mill to compete with the White-run mill that formerly constituted the only option for the local Black farmers; thus, the Bordelon family's sugar business represents some degree of restitution for the injustices of slavery and subsequent enduring structures of inequality. *Queen Sugar* celebrates the poetic justice of Black-owned farms and mills producing sugar, frequently reminding viewers that the people who worked those fields in past – including the Bordelon family's ancestors – were themselves treated as commodities. Up against the local White power structure, including the corrupt police force and local government, and armed with Charley's business acumen, Nova's skills as an investigative journalist and organizer, and Ralph Angel's hands-on farming experience, the Bordelons emerge as underdog challengers and symbolic avatars of racial justice in the fraught Louisiana landscape. Cane farming, in its first two centuries, was only viable due to the availability of enslaved laborers, and visible vestiges of the plantation system remain in the series, with wealthy White businesses still controlling much of the sugar industry in the parish. Explicit historical resonances in *Queen Sugar* among the institutions of slavery, sharecropping, and the contemporary hindrances still facing rural Black Americans provide otherwise-rare opportunities for reflection as, until recently, most Black screen settings have been urban or suburban (in this way the series resonates with the rural-set film *Fast Color*, discussed in the next section).

Queen Sugar's visual aesthetics and this rural setting on a Black-owned cane farm in the context of the series' preoccupation with racial justice can be productively read through the climate unconscious. I construe the "natural" beauty of the cane fields in *Queen Sugar*'s iconic landscape shots as part of the "banal Anthropocene," a term anthropologist Heather Anne Swanson coins in her observations about the pasts and present occluded in similar views in her home state:

When my uncle, a farmer in northeast Iowa, gazes out at his cornfields, he does not see the annihilation of the prairie, the loss of the bison, or the displacement of American Indian communities. He does not notice the contamination of the groundwater, even though he had to re-dig his well a few years ago due to bacterial seepage from a nearby pig farm. (Swanson 2017: n.p.; see also Leyda and Negra 2021)

Swanson's critique of the scholarship that frequently locates Anthropocene environmental destruction outside the everyday employs the notion of the banal to drive home, as it were, the way that American landscapes of the "heartland" have also been sculpted by the global dynamics of colonialism, extractivism, and toxicity. And while the Iowa farmlands she describes bear little trace of colonial and genocidal histories, the visual iconography of the Louisiana cane field in *Queen Sugar* explicitly summons up cultural memories of its blood-soaked pasts, conjuring a variation of Swanson's banal Anthropocene that is indeed marked by Blackness (see Figure 1).

Enslaved workers on that land were seen as what anthropologist David Hughes calls the "human, somatic fuel" that supported the global sugar industry, the Black bodies that constituted the vital foundation for the "energy without conscience" that drove the brutal economic engines of the plantation South and Caribbean (2017: 36). He identifies the amoral, instrumentalist discourses within the institutions of slavery that figured humans themselves as energy resources – this was "the lasting innovation of plantation slavery: a cultural understanding of production through long-distance, high-volume energy transport" (40). As Yusoff argues, slavery has been one of the primary engines of the Anthropocene: a "racialized equation of energy" central to "the movement between enslaved bodies in plantations, plants, long-dead fossilized plants, and industrialized labor" (2018: 16). *Queen Sugar* in its present-day setting performs constant callbacks to the ancestors as it asserts the Bordelon family's rightful place as owners of the farm (see Figure 1). Images of Ralph Angel in the lush, green cane fields visually allude to centuries of iconography while at the same time revising them to a picture of a farmer working his own land. As he and the other workers endure the subtropical heat of the late summer cane harvest, soaked in sweat and exhausted by the demanding work conditions, viewers can easily draw on common knowledge of how his ancestors performed similar labor, albeit without farm machinery or the mantle of freedom, much less proprietorship.

Visual images of the sweaty work of cane farming in *Queen Sugar* are an example of what I have elsewhere called the "premediation of a post-air-conditioning future," exemplified in shows such as *Daredevil* and *Dexter* (Leyda 2021: 104). My analysis of those series argues that their affective representation of extreme heat "prompts American viewers to imagine themselves in such inhospitable, un-climate-controlled environments" that may well await them in the climate-changed future (103). And while those other series depend on genre-appropriate affective scenarios of anxiety, dread, and fear circulating around their White/cis-male protagonists as analogues to the ambient climate anxiety in which many viewers are already steeped, the family drama *Queen Sugar* notably fosters a sense of hope, resistance, and collective struggle through its visual style, its family and community narrative focus, and its Black production context. Like *Fast Color* and its departure from the conventional imaginaries of cli-fi, which I discuss in the next section, *Queen Sugar* exemplifies feminist geographers Mabel Gergan, Sara Smith, and Pavithra Vasudevan's call for environmental storytelling that "render[s] clear how the lexicon of humanity has always been based on exclusionary racial violence and logics" (2020: 103). The setting of a Louisiana cane farm for a contemporary Black family drama reinscribes an alternative storyline and affective scenario onto that already rich narrative ground, without eliding the historical or contemporary traces of White supremacy that such a setting already bears in American cultural memory. The echoes of the plantation past are strategically positioned as both callbacks to familiar history and iconography and, simultaneously, as stark contrasts with the successes of the Bordelons in the present day.

Although the show's narrative briefly mentions organic farming practices and fracking, it mostly steers clear of overtly environmental issues, also eliding any mention of the health hazards associated with cane-farming practices (see Ramadan, Ngu, and Miller 2021). However, a climate-unconscious reading opens up several interpretive pathways and affective ecologies in *Queen Sugar*. The hum of the air conditioning and the traces of sweat remind us that Louisiana, like the rest of the Southern United States, has often been an inhospitable climate both literally and figuratively.[6] The Louisiana setting already calls to mind recent cultural memories of highly mediated anthropogenic catastrophes, including the 2005 inundation of New Orleans due to levee failures after Hurricane Katrina and the slow-motion nightmare of the 2010 Deepwater Horizon blowout in the Gulf of Mexico, the largest leak in petroleum industry history.[7] The legacies of Katrina and its brutal revelation of systemic

---

[6] At the time of writing in summer 2021, a record-smashing heatwave was baking northwestern North America, causing droughts, wildfires, and excess deaths, and proving that the South is not the only region that will be imperiled in the climate-changed future (see Brownstein 2021).

[7] *Queen Sugar* rarely touches on oil, a much more lucrative Louisiana industry than sugar, and one whose history has led to the observation that in its uneven development, Louisiana's oil and gas economy resembles an internal colony in which not only resources but also profits are exported.

racism surface in "Where with All" (S1 E8), as a hurricane approaches and sets in motion the post-traumatic responses of several characters. Building sympathy for Nova, who had broken her way out of her attic to escape the post-Katrina flooding as did many Black New Orleanians, the episode also casts farm boss Charley in a critical light for refusing to allow field workers to leave early to prepare for the storm. *Queen Sugar* portrays myriad other instances of laboring Black bodies at risk, including the suspenseful sequence in "To Usward" (S2 E2) when Aunt Violet (Tina Lifford) waits anxiously to see whether her boyfriend has survived a workplace accident on an offshore oil rig. The constant low-level dread of Black death is part of the climate unconscious as it permeates the everyday experience of the Bordelons, their employees, and their neighbors. These brushes with environmental catastrophes (exacerbated by the oil industry) exemplify the complex way *Queen Sugar*'s ensemble cast develops the show's overarching theme of strength in collectivity: Its multivocal stories narrate the community's constant state of conflict and resolution, modeling forms of resilience that could make it possible to both resist racism and survive the post-air-conditioning Deep South.

The climate unconscious of *Queen Sugar*'s balmy subtropical setting combines with its frequent allusions to slavery and plotlines about ongoing structural racism to open up a space for this Black drama's affective and aesthetic world-making. Adopting this reading strategy places the show in a framework that is not only inextricably bound up with Christina Sharpe's argument that America exists within a total climate of anti-Blackness but also does not omit acknowledgment of environmental crisis in the formation of the nation (Sharpe 2016: 111). The narrative demands of its genre shape *Queen Sugar* in its extended, interlocking storylines of grief, ambition, and love; as a Black family drama, those stories often also reckon with the anti-Black atmospheres as well as the Anthropocene ecologies in which the Bordelons live. These storylines and affective scenarios rely on audiences' ability to tap into contemporary structures of feeling surrounding the role of community in surviving both climate crisis and White supremacy.

2.2 Vibranium and Black Speculative Power in *Black Panther*

Black Panther has made an indelible mark on global popular culture. As of this writing, the movie ranks #4 in the all-time US box office, grossing over $1.3 billion worldwide (#12 in the all-time box office). Media responses to the movie present an impressive array of arguments and interpretations related to the politics of African (American) representation, aesthetics, and popular culture. *Black Panther*'s success sparked a heightened interest in Afrofuturism:

"speculative fiction that treats African American concerns in the context of 20th-century technoculture – and, more generally, African American signification that appropriates images of technology and a prosthetically enhanced future" (Dery 1994: 180). Cultural critic Ytasha Womack elaborates: "Both an artistic aesthetic and a framework for critical theory, Afrofuturism combines elements of science fiction, historical fiction, speculative fiction, fantasy, Afrocentricity, and magic realism with non-Western beliefs" (2013: 12). But even the most superficial search of the term reveals a transmedia phenomenon that encompasses fiction, comics, music, photography, painting, architecture, fashion, and more. *Black Panther* folds many of those modes of expression into its world-building and *mise-en-scène*, including the work of the first Black women to win Academy Awards for costume design (Ruth E. Carter) and production design (Hannah Beachler), whose richly researched work reflects Afrofuturism's emphasis on honoring African ancestors and facing the future with self-determination and innovation (see Figure 2). At a meta level, then, the commitment to hiring Black artists off-screen has played a role in propelling Carter and Beachler, and many more, into the limelight for their work on the film. The legacy of *Black Panther* will be enduring and far-reaching across film studies and cultural studies for years to come.

The film has received accolades for Carter's and Beachler's visually detailed world-building as displayed in its fictional African setting of Wakanda, a hidden high-tech utopia insulated from colonialism and slavery thanks to its unique domestic extraction industry, which is shrouded in secrecy. The quasi-magical mineral, vibranium, derived from a meteor crash in Wakandan territory, constitutes the basis for the kingdom's economy and development: It can be used as

Figure 2 *Black Panther*'s (2018) intricate world-building displays the Afrofuturist utopia of a high-tech, sustainable Wakanda, where vibranium constitutes the basis for a prosperous economic and spiritual life

energy source, building material, and weaponry, as well as an extremely lucrative natural resource in a strictly controlled export market. Science-fiction
writer Tochi Onyebuchi nails it: "Wakanda grows – in the absence of plunder,
in the absence of white avarice, in the absence of unadulterated capitalistic
impulses married to race hatred – into a wonderland. A marvel of technological
innovation. As though to say, this is what Africa would have become had you
not spoiled it" (2018: n.p.) (see Figure 2). Based on a comics series that started
in 1966, *Black Panther* features a brother-and-sister team as its protagonists:
Shuri, a brilliant scientist, and her brother, T'Challa, the Black Panther (see
Thomas 2018). Together they defend Wakanda from external threats and
internal discord: "*Black Panther* is a fantasy about Black power" (Newkirk
2018). That power resides in the political sphere and as literal energy: This
analysis homes in on the Black-owned power source on which Wakanda is built,
vibranium.

While vibranium is not the most prominent theme of the movie, the paradoxes surrounding it exemplify what popular culture texts can contribute to
current conversations about environmentalism and inequality. Reading *Black
Panther* as an Afrofuturist extractivist text, I heed literary scholar André
Carrington's call to complicate science fiction's "presumptive association
with Whiteness by forwarding examples in which Blackness is not an alienated,
exceptional quality but something integral" (2016: 21). My reading furthers that
aim while also assessing how the film's speculative depiction of extractivism
tugs at the climate unconscious, enabling a complementary interpretation of the
film that does not minimize the importance of its contributions to Black popular
culture, but situates it in an environmental framework in which too few Black
texts have been included, and where it has much to offer. Although most
audiences will experience *Black Panther* as a film about Black power both
behind and in front of the camera, both its narrative, premised on the sustainable
resource vibranium, and its affective scenarios valorizing the strength and
resistance found in family and community (as in *Queen Sugar*) also recall the
histories of climate justice movements around the world.

The fictional nation of Wakanda, untouched by colonialism and innocent of
complicity in the origins of the Anthropocene, operates a seemingly clean and
sustainable extraction industry fueling a prosperous independent society whose
"good life" depends on neither genocide nor environmental degradation.
Indigenous environmental historian Kyle Powys Whyte demonstrates the cocon-
stitution of colonialism with industrial capitalism in the real world: "As a means
of carving out settler homelands from indigenous homelands, waves of settlers
harnessed industrial means, from military technologies to large-scale mineral and
fossil fuel extraction operations to sweeping, landscape-transforming regimes of

commodity agriculture" (Whyte 2017: 208). Wakanda's extractivist society plays directly against what audiences already know about globalized extraction industries in real countries, such as those exporting fossil fuels, timber, or rare minerals, or those developed into plantation and other farming economies of scale (as discussed in the previous section). Those extraction industries literally fuel the single greatest environmental issue of our time: climate change.

Across the humanities and social sciences, histories of extraction foreground the intersections between environmental damage and social inequality; to take a recent event heavily covered in the world media, the Dakota Access Pipeline protests in North Dakota featured the mostly Native American community's struggle against the building of a pipeline forced upon them by the state in league with transnational capital (Streeby 2017). The protest's international media attention and public solidarity statements from Indigenous groups around the world, as well as Black Lives Matter and other antiracism movements, further underscored the dual crisis demanding the protection of both communities of color and the environment from the well-established dangers of the extraction industries. From Nigeria to China to Brazil to the Gulf of Mexico to the Arctic, extractivism has established roots in global and local economies and simultaneously spawned powerful global and local resistance movements. In addition to *Black Panther*'s alternate history narrative that spares Wakandans the Middle Passage, its utopianism reimagines, via Afrofuturism and vibranium, all-too-familiar exploitative extractivist scripts (see Figure 3).

Focusing on extractivism means exposing and rejecting oversimplifications of the concept of the Anthropocene that erase inequalities – the attitude that "we" humans have caused climate change on such a scale that it has altered the geologic record, without specifying which humans (wealthier ones) that "we" refers to, as opposed to which humans (poorer ones) most often suffer the

Figure 3 Vibranium mines in Wakanda enable its independence and stability and portray a benign form of extractivism in its Afrofuturist utopia

everyday consequence. As Imre Szeman asserts, "extraction needs to be a part of any and every account of our neoliberal present and of the politics required to address its inequalities and injustices" (2017: 445). Thus, attention to extractivism and other forms of what Rob Nixon (2011) calls "slow violence" reveals the unequal worldwide distribution of not only wealth but of damage and risk. African thinkers since Walter Rodney (1972) have linked European underdevelopment via extraction, slavery, and colonialism with subsequent African struggles against corruption, authoritarianism, and poverty; Naomi Klein extends and builds on those arguments to demonstrate global neoliberal patterns of crisis exploitation in her 2008 landmark theory of disaster capitalism, *The Shock Doctrine*. Extractivism has accompanied and exacerbated uneven capitalist development for centuries, with very few exceptions (as other sections will demonstrate, Norway makes an interesting contrast case). Enter Wakanda.

Vibranium is the high-tech beating heart of Wakanda and the source material for Shuri's inventions: weapons and armor (including Captain America's shield), transportation technology, energy sources, and medicine (see Figure 3). It is also at the center of Wakandan national and spiritual identity, as literary scholar Cathy Thomas observes: "Vibranium sutures technology to spirituality .... All Black Panthers get their abilities by ingesting a sacred mutagenic plant, the Heart-Shaped Herb, imbued with vibranium" (2018: 79). The imaginary substance, delivered from the skies early in Wakandan history, allows this fictional nation to escape the nightmares of White (neo)colonialism that ravage(d) much of Africa. As Ava DuVernay aptly observes, this fiction's premise hits hard for descendants of the African diaspora: "At the heart of Wakanda ... lie some of our most excruciating existential questions: What if they didn't come? ... And what if they didn't take us?" (Wallace 2018). To imagine what that alternative present would look like, *Black Panther* devises a secretive African nation that is economically self-sufficient thanks to vibranium. The utopian premise of Wakanda enacts what Carrington uncovers in his analysis of African American *X-Men* character Storm: "utopian interventions in popular culture have sometimes renovated problematic stereotypes by envisioning them under conditions that promise to enrich the cultural lexicon with expanded possibilities for the meaning of marginalized identities" (Carrington 2016: 92).[8] These expanded possibilities in *Black Panther* include new, futuristic framings for Black achievement and independence, with alternative energy figured as a valued part of both the socioeconomic commons and the spiritual life of Wakanda. As Thomas observes of the half-century-long history of *Black Panther* comics, culminating in the film: "The cultural work of Afrofuturism,

---

[8] In the Marvel comics, Storm also marries (and divorces) Black Panther.

Black feminist thought, intellectual activism, and intentional diversity has been a necessary part of the Black comic book tradition in the United States, and now its record of resistance is global" (2018: 91). That a central part of this global blockbuster's cultural work involves a utopian rewriting of a familiar extractivism narrative adds yet another epistemological layer onto the project of studying this landmark film and comics series.

The seeming absence of pollution, exploitation, and inequality in Wakanda inarguably presents a utopian model for an extraction economy that prioritizes the collective security and prosperity of its citizens: a harmonious Afrofuturist extractivist utopia (see Figure 3). The historical near-certainty that any developing nation that possesses something valuable will fall prey to external exploitation and/or domestic corruption – the so-called resource curse – informs *Black Panther*'s utopian vision, but it is constructed in defiance of that knowledge, in resistance to those histories, such that viewers may imagine that another world is possible. Analyzing the resource-curse concept and its limitations, Janet Stewart points out that "[u]nderstanding oil and other fossil fuels primarily as resources is part of the general disposition toward nature at the heart of global capitalism" (2017: 287). The Wakandan reverence for vibranium as more than a raw material – as a central agent of spirituality, providing access to the ancestors and consecrating their leaders as Black Panthers – revises the instrumentalist extraction narrative and invests vibranium with a value beyond the economic. That this fictional resource originated from outer space only underscores the degree to which vibranium is a fantasy; the real-life resources in many real African nations (like oil, diamonds, and rare minerals) pose more complicated dilemmas, not only in wealth distribution but in the toxic results of their local extraction and global use.

Far from a resource curse, vibranium in *Black Panther* enables Wakanda to maintain its sovereignty and avoid the hazards that have befallen so many resource-rich non-Western countries (and territories within Western countries), and political thinkers are paying attention. Taking the film's politics seriously, Florida Congressional representative Val Demmings held a Congressional Black Caucus panel on STEM (science, technology, engineering, and mathematics) and *Black Panther*, where director Ryan Coogler compared "Wakanda's relationship with vibranium to the Congo's relationship with the mineral coltan in the real world" (Johnson 2017). In *Foreign Policy* magazine, Jennifer Williams argues that *Black Panther*'s Afrofuturism, and in particular the portrayal of its tech sector based on vibranium, prompts geopolitical reassessments: "Africa is rich in mineral resources that are valuable to our tech-heavy futures – resources that foreign powers currently covet and expropriate. Yet it is also rich in innovative thinking that gets over-shadowed by the stereotypes of primitiveness, overpopulation, and despair" (2018: n.p.). The film's utopian imagery and its allusions to historical Black liberation movements push audiences to recognize the still-widespread ethno-centrism with which much of the world views the African continent, and to speculate about what would happen if the wealth and power generated by extraction industries there were allocated differently.

The climate unconscious as manifested in *Black Panther*'s Afrofuturist aesthetics and epistemologies weaves together audience awareness of envir-onmental realities (global heating, toxicity, inequalities in wealth and suffer-ing) with an invitation not to forget ugly realities but to imagine otherwise. Fans, film critics, and academics have lauded *Black Panther* as a "breakthrough in Black cultural representation," an allegory of African and African American self-determination, and "a glittering, cinematic maroon colony to which, for a few hours at least, we can all escape" (Connolly 2018). The complex ways the film mobilizes characterizations, storylines, settings, and aesthetics in service of an explicitly Black cultural politics bear out political scientist Alex Zamalin's assertion that "Black utopia was never a transhistorical idea," but rather exists "in conversation with prevailing political realities, crises, and cultural trends" including "the experience of enslavement, global empire, and the formative role of Enlightenment idealism and its radical offshoots" (2019: 10). Across 500 years of Black liberation struggles, storytelling has served as a central means of imagining an autono-mous future and keeping alive cultural memory, including memory of utopias: "what's most real about *Black Panther* are its literary and historical sinews tying us back into the Black past, or better to Black past *dreams*," writes historian N. D. B. Connolly (2018).

Dreams of the future are a key component in this film's utopian premise, and in Afrofuturism more generally. As Michael Bennett (2018: n.p.) observes, Wakanda is a high-tech, independent Black utopia that also seems to have solved other tenacious problems: "*Black Panther* challenges Afrofuturists to imagine worlds brimming with thriving Black people, applied knowledge production systems free of gross gender biases, and large-scale energy, trans-port, and food-production systems." Seeing such a fictional future world and taking visual pleasure in its articulation fosters what Sarah Jaquette Ray lists as a requirement for surviving the climate crisis: "We must maintain our motivation to keep desiring the future and keep working to create the condi-tions that will make that future not just tolerable, but worth living for" (2020: 126). Screen fictions like this activate the climate unconscious as part of their imaginative project, and as social psychologist Denise Baden's research on environmental storytelling proves, the coming "transition to a sustainable society requires profound changes, but to imagine how all of these aspects can come together is currently the domain of creative fiction" (2018: n.p.). *Black Panther*'s Afrofuturist climate unconscious highlights the importance of community and storytelling both to Black cultural production and to imagining livable futures.

2.3 A Black Climate Unconscious

This section reads for the climate unconscious as a way to investigate the eco-affects of two US American screen fictions, *Queen Sugar* and *Black Panther*. Examining these two important texts through a dual lens of environmental humanities and Black media studies, I demonstrate the usefulness of the climate unconscious for analyzing films and television series that are not explicitly about the environment. The approach unpacks the implicit resonances of climate crisis in representations of the fraught racialized materiality of two of the primary engines of the Anthropocene: plantation agriculture and energy extraction. The Marvel blockbuster *Black Panther*'s inherently political utopianism folds together histories of race, extractivism, capitalism, and technology, while also demonstrating the imaginative power of global popular culture itself in today's media-convergent world. On the other hand, the woman-centered melodrama of *Queen Sugar* reveals the quiet power of invoking the pasts of the plantation South within a contemporary capitalist context in which a Black family descended from enslaved people reap the profits of the cane harvest.

In directing viewer attention to the below-the-radar operations of sugar cane's and vibranium's iconography and affective allusiveness, I have reframed theoretical concepts from environmental humanities in conversation, and at times confrontation, with Black media studies. Because they are associated with different genres and aimed at different audiences, reading *Queen Sugar* and *Black Panther* together helps to discern the presences of a Black climate unconscious that can aid in unpacking always already racialized Anthropocene mediations of plantation pasts and extractivist futures. Although one is a prestige realist melodrama presumed to have a niche audience and the other a speculative utopia that became an international blockbuster, these Black popular culture artifacts represent manifestations of global and local networks of anti-Blackness and anthropogenic environmental destruction. This section establishes that contemporary Black screen cultures offer a rich ground for investigations that can productively combine environmental humanities with media studies approaches.

3 Stormy Weather: Reading for Race and Generation in Cli-Fi 2.0

The weather necessitates changeability and improvisation; it is the atmospheric condition of time and place; it produces new ecologies.

Christina Sharpe[9]

Gloom and misery everywhere/Stormy weather, stormy weather/And I just can't get my poor self together/Oh, I'm weary all the time

Harold Arlen and Ted Koehler, "Stormy Weather" (1933)[10]

Weather is a rich concept that has long lent itself to metaphorical use in cultural expression – as in the title of this chapter, which refers to the classic 1933 torch-song standard "Stormy Weather," first performed by actor and singer Ethel Waters and later adopted as the title for the 1943 Hollywood movie starring Lena Horne. In her performance of the song at the Cotton Club, Waters famously eschewed literalizing special effects in stage design, insisting that the performance should skew metaphorical; it should "have more to do with human emotions and should be expressed that way instead of with noise-making machines to interpret the rumblings and rattlings of Old Mother Nature" (Vogel 2008: 99). *Stormy Weather* was one of several Black-cast films of the Classical Hollywood era; it showcases a pantheon of acting, singing, and dancing talent across generations, from Bill Robinson to Katherine Dunham. However, as a backstage musical set at a fictional Harlem nightclub, it was also "both the first and last explicit tribute to African American achievement during the studio era" (Trenka 2014: 109). The film's staging of the title song opens with the thunderstorm metaphor as an externalization of the turbulent romance between the leads. However, the number also incorporates modernist flourishes that point to a more widespread anguish, including Dunham's modern ballet interlude indebted to African and Caribbean dance. These formal complexities, embedded in the torch-song sequence, convey what performance studies scholar Shane Vogel describes, drawing on theorists Paul Gilroy (1995) and Angela Y. Davis (1998), as a specifically Black "topos of unsayability" in which "the expression and transmission of pained histories and experiences . . . are rendered unspeakable by both the historical conditions that produced them and the overwhelming heartache that they produce" (Vogel 2008: 101). The song's weather trope, as staged in the movie's title number, unfolds a literal rainstorm into layers of metaphor, signifying both individual anguish and the collective Black "weariness" that Vogel traces to Langston Hughes's blues-inspired poetry and beyond.

---

[9] Sharpe (2016): 106.

[10] The 1933 song has lyrics by Ted Koehler and music by Harold Arlen. For a detailed history of the song and its performances, see Vogel (2008).

I open with this example to establish a pattern: in this section about the climate unconscious as stormy weather, I analyze characters whose attunement to their emotions enables them to alter weather phenomena. Their individual strife fuels their powers, allowing them to act on their wider sense of obligation to a collective. Emotional turmoil in these examples stands for more than an individual's struggle or a hallmark of youth; both young protagonists are agents of change in a world almost destroyed by older generations. Viewed through the lens of the climate unconscious, these protagonists embody the insistent call to action publicized by the media attention to Swedish teen activist Greta Thunberg and the global Fridays for Future youth climate movement, young people taking action to help their communities and explicitly rejecting the passive victim roles that previous mediations have constructed for them. As Jessalynn Keller argues, Thunberg constitutes a threat because she "refuses to do what we have come to expect of girl activists who cross borders on our screens – making 'us' feel good about a future, and in this case, one that relies on the global use of fossil fuels" (2021: 683). The young people with magical, weather-influencing powers in this section rewrite their own roles and assert agency on behalf of their cohort; they are also hallmarks of a new generation of climate fiction that, in the context of the climate unconscious, decisively rejects the previous generation's failures.

Because weather and climate are closely related yet distinct terms, a brief digression to clarify their meanings will also allow me to specify how they pertain to my arguments about the climate unconscious. In daily life, individuals often notice and comment on weather – short-term fluctuations in temperature, humidity, precipitation, and wind strength. Extreme weather also falls into this category – referring to anomalous or unusual weather phenomena, including hurricanes, floods, droughts, wildfires, and record-setting temperatures. Perhaps because it refers to familiar lived experience, the metaphor of stormy weather conveys both sense memories of literal storms and tempestuous emotions such as anxiety, fear, melancholy, or disappointment that can accompany them. Climate, on the other hand, is defined by longer-term widespread patterns in weather phenomena based on accumulated data. The August 2021 report by the IPCC (IPCC 2021) indicates that human activity has already contributed to unprecedented and irreversible changes in the Earth's climate, sparking alarm at the dwindling timeframe available to take the action that is required to avoid worse. The relation between weather and climate, then, lies in temporality and scale – individuals cannot experience (or accurately recall) weather across the vast time periods and range of locations necessary to assess climate; they are limited to their own standpoints. Human control over weather is negligible, aside from localized practices such as cloud seeding to increase rain or snow (or, in these fictional protagonists, magical powers that allow them to alter weather conditions). Collective human influence on climate over longer periods, however, is proven by established science, and experts continue to urge immediate changes in human behavior to slow the pattern of global heating that is exacerbating the extreme weather disasters increasingly splashed across daily news reports. The climate unconscious, in an analogous way, stems from the general awareness most audiences carry around in the form of accumulated mediated knowledge of extreme weather events made worse by the ongoing climate crisis, and thus the (uneven) human culpability for both. In this sense, weather and climate have distinct definitions and usages, but are also often conflated as closely related terms.

In recent scholarly work, too, weather proves a durable trope in both Black studies and environmental humanities, making meaning on multiple levels. In her book *In the Wake: On Blackness and Being*, theorist Christina Sharpe (2016) builds a complex theory of anti-Blackness around a series of concepts and their broad usages: the wake, the ship, the hold, and the weather. The chapter on weather unpacks the way the term takes on an array of meanings and connotations in her ontological analysis of Blackness: as a noun, weather is related to both climate and environment while, as a verb, it signals endurance and survival. As in Waters's metaphorical interpretation of the song "Stormy Weather," Sharpe's weather is "not the specifics of any one event or set of events that are endlessly repeatable and repeated, but the totality of the environments in which we struggle" (111). For Sharpe, weather and climate serve as synonyms for environment or atmosphere, and as apt metaphors to express the experience of racism: "antiblackness is pervasive as climate. The weather necessitates changeability and improvisation; it is the atmospheric condition of time and place; it produces new ecologies" (106). Building on the affective dimensions of Sharpe's "weather" and reinscribing into the metaphor a material sense of the experience of (extreme) weather and climate (change), Astrida Neimanis and Jennifer Mae Hamilton argue that, for them, "weathering means learning to live with the changing conditions of rainfall, drought, heat, thaw, and storm as never separable from the 'total climate' of social, political, and cultural existence of bodies" (2018: 82). Their notion of weathering thus folds Sharpe's engagement with race into compelling interrogations of the Anthropocene concept that foreground the inequalities often smoothed over with the universalizing term.

Inspired by these multivalent usages of the concept of weather and its association with affect and emotion, this section delves into the climate unconscious in recent youth-centered screen climate fiction, or cli-fi. Without venturing too far into the weeds of debating the exact definition of cli-fi, for the purposes of this analysis, I simply mean "fictional texts, in print, in live performance, and on the screen, engaging with the local and global impact of advanced human-induced climate change" (Leikam and Leyda 2017: n.p.). In many mediations of the climate unconscious, extreme weather is not overtly linked to climate crisis but is portrayed in a way that rather resembles post-apocalyptic and disaster genres; it takes on a menacing agency that threatens human victims, whose main goals become surviving, escaping, and rescuing others. These on-screen framings of weather depend on affects such as fear, anxiety, and dread to propel their narrative; they also demand closer attention to racialization and the mobilization of affect in the storytelling and aesthetics. The examples I discuss in this section display novel developments in cli-fi, including protagonists who can, in fact, change the weather at will, while also framing weather as metaphorical, affective, and racialized.

Since its popularization in mainstream US American cinema in the early 2000s, cli-fi has relied on mostly White, mostly cis-male protagonists: in now-canonical cli-fi films like *The Day after Tomorrow* (2004) and *The Road* (2009), White cis-men occupy lead roles as heroic fathers – a configuration that, unlike in Hollywood's initial cycle of disaster films in the 1970s (one of the precursor genres for cli-fi), frequently fails to contest the social formations that (in)directly led to the disasters in the first place (Leyda and Loock 2022). Cli-fi as an emergent genre, like (post-)apocalyptic screen stories, tended to stumble on the move from individual to collective rescues, figuring the often White, often male, often US American leads as the heroes while overlooking the stories of most "others" in the resolution of crisis. Mainstream-media represen-tations of future crisis, including extreme weather linked (overtly or not) to anthropogenic climate crisis, portray social worlds that "have often been framed through an exclusionary hierarchy of humanity, necessitating closer examin-ation of how clichéd genre conventions that saturate our media environment rely on anti-Black racism and Indigenous erasure" (Gergan et al. 2020: 92). Moreover, while conventions of postapocalyptic and cli-fi screen media regu-larly elide Black and Indigenous experience, they also often naturalize Whiteness as the unmarked norm among those empowered to rescue others.

Analyzing the White/father-hero trope, gender studies scholar Barbara Gurr emphasizes the importance of attending to social hierarchies of race, gender, and other power relations in screen imaginaries of the (re)construction of future societies in the aftermath of disasters, or what she terms "the politics of the post-apocalypse" (Gurr 2015: 3). Diane Negra and I note the father-hero and White-savior tropes, which often (but don't always) overlap, across a wide range of extreme weather films, from blockbuster to exploitation to art house, in which "conservative assumptions about race, class, and community shape ...

narratives" and "use disasters as proving grounds for paternal love and patriarchal power" (Leyda and Negra 2015: 4; see also Seymour 2013). Moreover, these paternalistic patterns persist in cli-fi that originates beyond North America: the Chinese film *The Wandering Earth* (2019) centers around a father's self-sacrifice to save his son and the Earth, while the South Korean dystopian action-comedy *Space Sweepers* (2021) features a father searching in vain for his adopted daughter and finding consolation in rescuing a young cyborg girl who can save the climate change–ravaged Earth in the year 2092. With minor variations, then, a discernable plot about fathers (and absent mothers) characterizes many cli-fi films, starting with the Anglophone canon that was first identified in early scholarly works on such films (Kaplan 2016; Svoboda 2016). And while some of that first cycle of cli-fi films did break out of the disaster/dystopian model and attempt greater diversity, with Black (*Beasts of the Southern Wild*, 2012) or nonhuman (*WALL-E*, 2008) protagonists, the preponderance of early cli-fi did not. Moreover, even those exceptions have been aptly critiqued for their uncritical recycling of racial, class, and gender stereotypes (Brown 2013; Sharpe 2013; Yates 2018).

Contemporary audiences increasingly expect more insightful and diverse futures, responding to much cli-fi popular culture with impatience, as Briggetta Pierrot remarks in an article coauthored with Nicole Seymour on Indigenous erasure in cli-fi novels: "Man, I'm tired of reading about white men saving the environment" (2020: 93). Pierrot echoes my own students' frustration with these prevalent clichés after watching several of the films in my cli-fi seminars in 2017 and 2018, in which White men frequently act heroically out of a motivation to save their children. In the spirit of Pierrot's lament, this section examines two notable departures from the now-tired convention: *Fast Color* (2018) and *Ragnarok* (2020–3) turn toward younger protagonists, one of whom is Black US American and the other White Norwegian. These two youths signal a discernable generational shift in cli-fi protagonists that extends beyond the normalized White/American/father and flips the young person's role from that of helpless victim awaiting rescue to powerful agent of change with the potential to save their communities and by extension the Earth. Moreover, this younger generation's ability to change the weather – to change the world, in the context of a climate crisis – further differentiates these protagonists from those of the earlier generation of the cli-fi genre, in which characters mostly had to react or adapt to, or escape or get rescued from, extreme weather that, although often shown as anthropogenic, was beyond human control.

The first cycle of cli-fi films (distinguished from books, which were more varied from the start) emerged just after the turn of the millennium and tended to fall into a similar pattern of shared genres, focalizations, and tropes. The most-referenced example is *The Day after Tomorrow*, along with successors including *Take Shelter* (2011) and *Interstellar* (2014). These movies tend to cluster within the disaster, postapocalyptic, science-fiction, and/or thriller genres, recycling familiar tropes. Among these are the Cassandra dilemma, in which nobody believes a character's predictions until it's too late, and the reproductive futurist trope of couching concerns for the future in terms of the plight of one's helpless offspring, rather than acting on a wider collective sense of obligation (Leyda 2018: 96–97; Seymour 2013: 7–9).

Although most cli-fi positions humans as victims of extreme weather, in the form of drought, floods, or tornadoes filled with sharks (Leyda and Negra 2015: 10–11), popular culture boasts several characters who can create or alter weather conditions: these include numerous superhero (and supervillain) figures such as the X-Men's Storm, for example, and Elsa in Disney's *Frozen* franchise. These characters from highly successful transmedial comics and children's animation presage the recent generic reconfiguration that I call cli-fi 2.0, whereby the conventional White US American nuclear family no longer dominates (Leyda 2020). This second cycle of films and series about climate change breaks with the first, although their chronologies overlap. In cli-fi 2.0, I locate those films and series that depart from that pattern in significant ways: the Swiss-German indie *Hell* (2011) and the Australian *Mad Max: Fury Road* (2015) in terms of focalization; other examples include US comedies such as the *Sharknado* franchise (2013–) and *Downsizing* (2017), and art-house films including *Kona fer í stríð [Woman at War]* (2018), a quirky Icelandic film centered around a single, middle-aged female activist, and *First Reformed* (2017), a dark US drama about a Protestant pastor. Some titles straddle both generations, but I find this schema useful for talking about general patterns across a burgeoning cluster of films and series.

In the cli-fi 2.0 case studies in this chapter, the focus falls on powerful young adults in lieu of paternalistic father figures, situated within a Black all-female multigenerational family in *Fast Color* and a White working-class, single-mother Norwegian household in *Ragnarok*, respectively (see Figure 4). The fathers in these stories are absent, marginal, or malevolent, while youths take center stage. Amid retreating glaciers, catastrophic drought, and tempestuous young-adult angst, these fictional screen texts stage circumstances in which the climate crisis not only affects, but can be mitigated by, people beyond the White American metropole. Significantly, these "misfit" characters emerge as active agents with fledgling magical abilities and a sense of obligation to aid not only their own families but wider collectivities. The climate unconscious moves into the spotlight in these screen fictions, whose narratives are explicitly about

Figure 4 The cli-fi film *Fast Color* (2018) focalizes three generations of rural Black women whose magical powers may hold the key to surviving a years-long drought.

weather and climate change, precisely because these self-reflexive, second-generation cli-fi texts improve upon their predecessors. By staging stories in which powerful protagonists learn to assume responsibility for their communities and choose to take decisive action to use their weather-modification powers to ameliorate some of the worst effects of climate change, *Fast Color* and *Ragnarok* convey the importance of youth agency in building inhabitable futures where awareness of climate crisis is no longer consigned to a textual unconscious.

3.1 Black Girl Magic Meets Cli-Fi 2.0 in *Fast Color*

Cut to a movie scenario: a young mixed-race woman surrounded by dry scrub in the southwestern United States, summoning lightning, thunder, clouds, and rain. Set in the near future, the film depicts Ruth (Gugu Mbatha-Raw) returning to her family's farm in a drought-scarred landscape, where her weather-creating superpowers first manifest in a cloudburst that yields the first rainfall in the area in eight years (see Figure 4). Ruth, a homeless recovering addict and single mother, belongs to a matriarchal line of Black women with magical powers: they are able to "take apart" solid objects that are thus reduced to dust-like particles, and to reassemble them again at will. In a departure from the saccharine father–daughter bonds at the center of so many cli-fi films (think *Interstellar*), Ruth's White father never becomes a hero, although he displays affection and loyalty to her and her mother. Rather, the film implies that Ruth's unique rain-making superpowers (literalizing the popular hashtag

#BlackGirlMagic) (Wilson 2016) may hold the key to alleviating the water shortages already endemic in the arid world of filmmaker Julia Hart's indie film *Fast Color*.

Focalizing three generations of Black women, *Fast Color* takes its place among a small number of nonpatriarchal cli-fi films,[11] although it is also often (mis)characterized as a superhero film, another recently diversifying genre that also occasionally overlaps with cli-fi. *Fast Color* poses a damning critique of the White male savior trope, and entirely discards the notion of science-based technofixes, casting a White male scientist, Bill (Christopher Denham), as an antagonist who attempts to trick, then kidnap, then blackmail Ruth into submitting to his research on her family's gifts. Following the instinct of most fictional characters with special powers, Ruth flees in justifiable fear that her human rights would not be respected were she to submit herself as test subject. Even if Bill could study the women and learn more about their powers, the unethical methods he displays do not justify any hope that (White) science will save the Earth from the drought. As a Black woman in particular, Ruth's fear makes sense given the medical profession's history of inhumane treatment of Black people, best known through the infamous cases of physician J. Marion Sims's nineteenth-century gynecological experiments on enslaved women and the twentieth-century Tuskegee Syphilis Study (Zhang 2018; Tuskegee Study 2020). These dreadful pasts surface often in popular culture, most recently in *Lovecraft Country*'s (2019–) haunted basement, where Lucy, Anarcha, and Betsey (the names of three of Sims's victims) lie buried; and in the Marvel Comics character, Isaiah Bradley, a Black man who has survived involuntary experimentation with early (deadly) versions of the super-soldier serum that created Captain America.[12] With its menacing White male scientist, *Fast Color* implicitly forecloses any faith in science for a technofix to solve climate change, instead elevating the embodied, ancestral female knowledge of magic as passed down through handwritten notes, personal tutelage, and covert alliances.

Fast Color complicates cinematic conventions further: instead of portraying a Black urban female-headed household as a source of instability and disadvantage, as has been common in mainstream representations at least since the

---

[11] Swiss–German indie film *Hell* (2011) broke new ground in its handling of cli-fi reproductive futurism: it follows the desperate journey of two sisters struggling to survive in a bleached-out, postapocalyptic Europe. When they are finally taken in (in more ways than one) by a dour Christian farm family, the film devolves into a cannibalistic horror movie, which, although generically disappointing, nevertheless also delivers a welcome critique, even with its entirely White cast, of cli-fi reprofuturism and family values. Like the blockbuster *Mad Max: Fury Road* (2015), *Hell* is set in a drought-ridden future where women save one another, with or without the help of men.

[12] Bradley appeared in the Marvel television series *The Falcon and the Winter Soldier* (2021).

Moynihan Report (1965) demonized single motherhood and absent fathers as causes of Black poverty, the film shows a self-sufficient farm family across three generations, in which magical powers are a matrilineal legacy (see Figure 4). At the same time, the film resists idealizing the Black "superwoman" stereotype by portraying the inner conflicts that drive Ruth's restlessness and addictions (Wallace 1978; Sulimma 2021: 177–180). Ruth's complex character also provides a welcome relief from the one-dimensional protagonists familiar to cli-fi audiences, and in its portrayal of her family, the film offers multiple Black female perspectives on power, family, and responsibility. However, Ruth has suffered from her own "stormy weather" throughout her young life: she has dangerous seizures that cause strong earthquakes. To protect those around her from harm, she ran away from home and took drugs to dampen her seemingly uncontrollable powers. Her mother Bo (Lorraine Toussaint) has raised Ruth's daughter Lila (Saniyya Sidney) in her absence, teaching her about her powers and keeping her safe on the family's isolated farm. After demonstrating that her magic allows her to escape at any time, thus obviating any possible captivity or control, Bo voluntarily agrees to work with the scientists if they agree to stop pursuing Ruth. The self-sacrifice of the mother (not the father) in *Fast Color* is thus presented as a willing cooperation, a strategy to facilitate Ruth's escape with Lila. Rather than simply flip the cli-fi cliché of the individual, nuclear family plot, which could show either (1) mother instead of father saving child, or (2) child rescuing parent for a change, the film shifts the power relations so that both mother and daughter (and granddaughter) can assert agency to salvage the Earth from climate change, and act to save not only a family member but a wider collective. Bo has told Ruth, in her childhood, stories of other women around the world with such powers, and the film hints at the coalitional possibilities as Ruth and Lila take to the road in the final scene, building expectations of possible sequels.

Fast Color represents a promising development in the screen politics of cli-fi representation: with Ruth, this unique indie film centers on a young Black woman who has weathered storms resulting from her formidable gift, and tracks her efforts to master it (see Figure 5). Her troubles rest in her own traumas of loss and addiction, yet her increasing agency offers hope to a wider world. Ruth admires Poly Styrene, the Somali-English frontwoman of the 1970s punk band X-Ray Spex, playing their music in one scene and quoting Styrene in another. As a mixed-race nonconformist female artist in a White-male-dominated sub-culture, Styrene represents Ruth's own difference: Ruth has a White father and her magic manifests in ways that differ from her mother's and daughter's. The film's references to Styrene hint at Ruth's agency and creativity as well as her punk-rock angst, constructing a rebellious but not ill-fated character. *Fast Color*

Figure 5 Ruth (Gugu Mbatha-Raw) in *Fast Color* stands in the desert and sees
for the first time the swirling colors that her magically gifted mother and
daughter have described to her as she discovers her ability to call forth rain

adeptly sidesteps the "tragic mulatto" stereotype that entraps many other light-complected Black characters even in otherwise innovative films: the unfortunate character who passes for White and thus loses first her place in her birth family and social world, and then (usually) her precarious position in a White milieu (see Bastiaans 2008). Ruth, in contrast, has no romantic relationships (doomed or otherwise) and her family ties are mended (not sundered) over the course of the film; her suffering is not caused by her mixed-race identity but rather by her struggle coming to terms with her substantial yet unwieldy power. Her story arc traces a difficult and not-yet-complete path to self-acceptance and reconciliation with her mother and daughter, which leads to her realization that she might be able to control her gift and use it to bring rain to the parched Earth. Indeed, the film itself represents hybridity in its racialized and gendered revision of cli-fi clichés, thematizing and portraying that which often goes unseen or unrepresented in contemporary speculative fiction: a young Black woman embodying environmentalist agency.

Beyond characterization and story, the film's aesthetic choices also set it apart from canonical cli-fi films: its setting in a remote drought-ridden farm town that resembles the White family-owned farm setting of *Interstellar* (see Figure 4). The film thus breaks the cinematic conventions that often place African American characters in urban locations. With its choice of setting, *Fast Color* participates in what film scholar Paula Massood has rightly characterized as an emerging shift beyond urban settings in twenty-first-century Black film, as the city increasingly "is a backdrop or absent altogether, and either suburban or rural spaces have replaced it." However, she points out that "[u]nlike decades before . . . these rural spaces in particular signify a contemporaneity rather than a static ahistoricity" (Massood 2003: 224). The novelty of seeing Black women at home in rural landscapes and locales operates as a reminder of both Black American rural pasts and of the paucity of screen images of contemporary (and near-future) rural Black life, which I also considered in my readings of *Queen Sugar* in the previous section. As in *Queen Sugar*, setting matters in *Fast Color*: the arid scrubland of what is currently the southwestern United States has been home to Indigenous and Latinx populations since before the nation existed, and is also currently facing increasingly hot, dry forecasts due to climate change (Hedden 2021). As another instance of the banal Anthropocene, the visual iconography of the desert bears inscriptions of its racialized histories and its possible climate futures.

In addition to the visual impact of its austere New Mexico landscapes and their traces of the climate unconscious, *Fast Color* employs striking special effects to illustrate the sublime beauty of magic rather than, as in earlier cli-fi films, to create terrifying computer-generated extreme weather or other disasters (see Figure 5). Approaching *Fast Color*'s aesthetics, I draw on film scholar Racquel Gates's point that critical conversations about visual pleasure have historically elided Black screen images, while at the same time studies of Black media have "been stuck circling around questions of representation rather than seeking to understand how they are created, exhibited, and circulated throughout the world" (2017: 40; 43–44). I concur with her argument that although recent turns toward technology and industry studies that examine race are necessary and important, "old-school" formalist film analysis has barely begun to acknowledge its own racial positionality, because it has traditionally focused on White film (broadly construed). Indeed, many of us in film and television studies are working to adopt a wider spectrum of complementary methods that allow a more complete critical conversation about Black screen aesthetics and politics: "Questions of style cannot be separated from questions of politics. Aesthetics bear the indelible imprint of racial ideologies" (44). The politics of visual style feature prominently in *Fast Color* in its striking portrayal of a young Black woman who can reverse a years-long drought with magic.

The aesthetic choices involved – spending an indie film's limited effects budget on shimmering clouds of color above a desert landscape instead of ice tsunamis or tornadoes lobbing sharks – simultaneously break new ground in the conventions of cli-fi and those of Black film (see Figure 5). If the colors in the sky that Ruth can summon are, as implied in the title, "fast" or permanent, then the sere high plains that dominate much of the film only show one way of seeing. When she uses her powers, Ruth conjures an aurora of rainbow swirls where most see only normal sky, indicating the importance of young people's and Black women's vision in the path to a livable climate future. Indeed, the film's title alludes to not only the rainbow-hued effects Ruth marshals with her magic but also the film's emphasis on women of color. Attending to the climate unconscious in *Fast Color* affords viewers a novel visual and affective experience of a possible future; in concert with the racialized layers of meaning inherent in the critical frame of stormy weather this section sets up, the film also provides a brilliant alternative glimpse of colors, characters, and futures usually occluded from cli-fi.

Ironically, the groundbreaking representational and aesthetic aspects of *Fast Color* are precisely the reasons why so few have seen it. Alongside my analysis of on-screen representation and aesthetics, the prevailing anti-Black and patriarchal climate in the film industry also bears closer scrutiny, as diversity behind the camera garners more public attention than ever before in the wake of the #metoo and #OscarsSoWhite phenomena. *Fast Color* is a cli-fi 2.0 example of the way concerns about the environment can coexist within a story primarily focused on Black women's power. Further, its industry context illuminates the obstacles that innovative work by women and filmmakers of color frequently faces. The film's disappointing performance at the box office, according to White filmmaker Julia Hart, resulted from enduring White male power hierarchies in the film industry, where "there is so much lip service … about wanting women to tell stories, wanting people of color to tell stories" that doesn't get backed up in practice (Gardner 2019: n.p.).[13] Hart explains that, when she shopped around, she found that although many executives were enthusiastic about the film, "when it got to the white male gatekeeper – time and time again – they said, 'I don't know who this movie is for.'" Even after the film was picked up, and even with a White (albeit female) filmmaker behind it, it received only a limited release and no print ad campaign.

Kristen Warner points out that "actual progress" in the systemic racism inherent in the media industries will require those industries to move beyond the surface "visual diversity" that she terms "plastic representation," exemplified by the increasing implementation of "colorblind casting." Warner argues that such progress can only occur with far-reaching structural shifts in the industry toward "a more weighted diversity, one generated by adding dimension and specificity to roles, and achieved in tandem with diverse bodies shaping those roles at the level of producing and writing" (2017: 35). *Fast Color* clearly faced obstacles because of its diversity and the lack of commitment that allowed it to languish with such a tepid release strategy. However, for its television adaptation

---

[13] With its White woman director, *Fast Color* does not meet the definition of a "Black film" in every sense. However, because the primary characters are all Black women, this section treats *Fast Color* as such in terms of on-screen representations.

(in development for Amazon, which now also holds streaming rights for the film), *Fast Color* has found a more nurturing home at Viola Davis's production company JuVee, with the original filmmaker and cast involved.[14] Like Ava DuVernay's company Array (discussed in the previous section), JuVee aims to build "a new and safe ecosystem that embraces all points of view as equals so that the artists can create [a] paradigm shift in the industry."[15] As both aesthetics and politics continue to shape the interests of Black film studies and environmental humanities, there is reason to hope that Black and female executives and creatives will continue to wield more power in the screen industries, providing a more welcoming climate for a new generation of more diverse cli-fi.

Asserting control over the weather, using her power to contribute to a more hospitable climate, *Fast Color*'s young Ruth is literally a rainmaker in a time of drought. The film departs from the standard set of cli-fi clichés through its diverse casting, its rejection of reproductive futurism and White-male-hero-driven technofixes, and its centering on the agency, rather than victimhood, of a youthful protagonist. Further, the film's ethereal aesthetic makes a strong counterexample when read alongside the typical cli-fi reliance on spectacular-ized catastrophes and related affects of fear and dread. Stormy weather, in Ruth's case, refers to both her personal struggles and subsequent triumphs as she masters her magic to fight the drought. Weathering is an apt concept for the film, in Sharpe's (2016) sense as well as Neimanis and Hamilton's (2018); the film champions survival despite the anti-Black atmospheres that many gener-ations of Ruth's family have faced, as well as the privations of climate change of which the enduring drought is a sign. Reading *Fast Color* through the lens of a Black climate unconscious opens it to a political analysis not only of racialized and gendered representation and industry dynamics, but also of the politics of climate crisis on screen.

3.2 Transnational Mediation of White Ethnic Cli-Fi in *Ragnarok*

In the pilot episode of *Ragnarok*, blond Norwegian teenager Magne (David Stakston) watches helplessly as his best friend parasails down a mountain and into a powerline, sending a shower of sparks bursting across the fjord (see Figure 6).

[14] JuVee is also developing a biopic about Black American activist-politician Shirley Chisholm, and adapting Black science-fiction novelist Octavia Butler's novel *Wild Seed* for television (Andreeva and Petski 2019).

[15] JuVee Productions. "About." www.juveeproductions.com/about/. Davis's 2015 Emmy accept-ance speech called out the need for a paradigm shift: "The only thing that separates women of color from anyone else is opportunity. You cannot win an Emmy for roles that are simply not there." Thanks to Maria Sulimma for reminding me of this speech. ("Viola Davis' emotional acceptance speech" *BBC News* [2015, September 21]. www.bbc.com/news/entertainment-arts-34312420.)

Figure 6 In the pilot episode of *Ragnarok* (2020–), Magne (David Stakston) witnesses the electrocution of his friend Isolde (Ylva Bjørkaas Thedin) as she parasails across the iconic Norwegian snowy mountain landscape, occasioning an intense emotional response that summons a thunderstorm (S1E1 "New Boy").

As he sobs, clutching Isolde's (Ylva Bjørkaas Thedin) lifeless body, peals of thunder punctuate the musical score's lament, indicating stormy weather approaching. Over the course of the series, Magne discovers that he is an avatar of the Norse god Thor, protector of humankind who controls thunder and storms, and that extreme emotions activate his powers. Inspired by his close friendship with the late eco-activist Isolde and her love for Norway's idyllic landscapes, he assumes her mantle as an environmentalist agitator fighting to expose ecocrime and demand stronger regulations to preserve local glaciers and drinking water.[16] As in *Fast Color*, weather-controlling superpowers are at the center of Norway-set fantasy series *Ragnarok*, in which Magne takes up an epic struggle against evil *jotner* (adversaries of the gods).[17] Staging his confrontation with these antagonists, embodied by the wealthy industrialist Jutul family, who employ most of the town

---

[16] Lesbian character Isolde conforms to the enduring TV tropes of "Bury Your Gays" and the "Disposable Woman," dying in the series pilot and existing only as an inspiration for Magne's heroism. However, at least her characterization departs from cli-fi clichés in that Magne is motivated by their strong platonic bond, rather than the White male hero's usual romantic or parental relationship. See "Bury Your Gays" (https://tvtropes.org/pmwiki/pmwiki.php/Analysis/BuryYourGays) and "Disposable Woman" (https://tvtropes.org/pmwiki/pmwiki.php/Main/DisposableWoman) in *TV Tropes*.

[17] The Norwegian *jotun* (singular) and *jotner* (plural) are translated as "giant" in the English subtitles, and *jotner* in Norse myth are often giant-sized. However, the term's meaning is more complicated; some *jotner* are beautiful and clever. In the series, the Jutul family of *jotner* are not large or ugly like the "giant" of English-language folk tales; the word *jotun* is also sometimes translated to mean troll, and they are often compared to the Titans of Greek mythology. In the Marvel transmedia universe, they are called Frost Giants (see Næss 2020).

including Magne's mother, the series transposes an ancient mythological conflict to contemporary Norway. The Jutul business pollutes the region's groundwater and contributes to climate change, made visible by a nearby melting glacier and local news stories about undrinkable tap water and unseasonable weather phenomena. Magne mourns Isolde (murdered by the Jutul paterfamilias, in an interesting twist on the usually heroic cli-fi father), taking on the villains to save Norwegian nature and thereby setting up a narrative of stormy weather similar to that in *Fast Color*: turbulent personal emotions catalyze the young person's weather-controlling powers, which they employ in defense of the collective good.

Whereas *Fast Color* breaks with earlier cli-fi conventions by casting a young Black US American woman as protagonist, *Ragnarok* stars a White Norwegian, modifying the usual White male father-hero role into a working-class teen with learning difficulties and a single mother. His conflict with the Jutuls also situates contemporary environmentalism in the long cultural heritage of Norse myth and Norwegian nationalism, both in the show's storyline and its iconic setting. *Ragnarok* draws its title from the Old Norse word for the battle that leads to end of the world, a signal that the series depends on its global audience having a smattering of cultural knowledge about Norse mythology. It lays on Norse allusions and iconography so heavily that most viewers will recognize at least some of them, if, for example, they follow the Marvel's Thor character (from 2017's *Thor: Ragnarok* perhaps) or the historical fantasy series *Vikings* (2013–20), or even, at the other end of the cultural spectrum, the operas of Richard Wagner's Ring cycle (Magne's friend Isolde's opera-fan father named her after the heroine of Wagner's 1865 *Tristan and Isolde*). Magne wields a hammer and summons thunder, a disabled, eye-patch-sporting elder embodies Odin, and, in the second season, Magne's queer half-sibling Laurits (Jonas Strand Gravli) comes out as trickster god Loki. *Ragnarok* deploys Norway's heritage – its mythology and its cultural reverence for sublime nature – in tandem with the climate unconscious, predicated on what audiences already know about the contemporary climate crisis from news media. In what follows, I think through the contemporary paradoxes behind the show's Whiteness to uncover how the climate unconscious operates in the mediated context of racialized Norwegianness.

The series is explicitly designed as an export for Netflix's international audience, and thus the wider media image of Norway plays into the mobilization of the climate unconscious. As the third "Norwegian" Netflix production (after the fish-out-of-water mixed-language comedy *Lillyhammer* [2012–14] and über-hygge seasonal romcom *Hjem til ju /Home for Christmas* [2019–20]), *Ragnarok* is heavily invested in projecting an imaginary Norwegianness for foreign viewing pleasure. It enjoys relative success globally: it was renewed for a third season, slated for release in 2023. Add in the show's on-the-nose environmentalist angle as a timely selling point and the rugged landscapes as eye candy, and Netflix appears to have created a successful series. Indeed, the uniformly negative critical reception of *Ragnarok* in Norway (population 5.3 million) is barely relevant for a Netflix Original Series because the global streaming service stands to profit primarily from marketing the Nordic show to those outside the region.

However, the local grumbling deserves a moment of consideration because it, perhaps improbably, recalls critiques of screen representation in other contexts, including those around race in the United States. *Ragnarok* has met with harsh reviews at home for a variety of failings, including its implausible mishmash of regional accents, its blatant imitation of national public broadcaster broadcaster NRK's smash teen drama *Skam* (2015–17), and its Danish showrunner and production company (Nilsen 2020; Thorvik 2020). While valid, these criticisms are grounded entirely in the domestic context; most viewers outside Norway would not notice these issues at all or would find them unproblematic. Moreover, this local appetite for Norwegian authenticity, while understandable, also recalls ongoing debates in Black film and media studies around accurate representation and the need for more complex analysis of what Gates calls the "racialized politics of aesthetics" (2017: 38). Although not equivalent, echoes of authenticity critique in many of the negative reviews of *Ragnarok* reveal a sensitive Norwegian identity politics bristling at linguistic inaccuracies and incongruous staffing decisions. While outsiders (correctly) see Norway as a wealthy country in the Global North, Norwegians are still prone to indignation over perceived misrepresentations in the few occasions their small country is portrayed in global media. After all, when a group of people are so rarely represented, every instance matters to them.[18] However, this series deserves more nuanced interrogations that take into account aesthetics as well as other kinds of politics, beyond inter-Scandinavian disputes, not least environmental politics and the politics of Whiteness.

Amplified by its entanglement in romantic imaginaries of Norwegian national nature, *Ragnarok* exemplifies how Whiteness is both unmarked and foregrounded in Norwegian eco-dramas, which capitalize on historically successful region-branding clichés endemic to Nordic screen exports (Jacobsen 2018). As a regional export, *Ragnarok* fits TV scholar Jakob Stougaard-Nielsen's observation that the early twenty-first-century television export boom in Nordic noir participates in a form of White nostalgia, whereby bourgeois UK audiences consume Nordic White ethnicity along with the shows (Stougaard-Nielsen 2016: 3–4). Nordic Whiteness provides US and UK

---

[18] I'm grateful to Nina Lager Vestberg for helping me tease out this point.

audiences, in whose popular television Whiteness is often unmarked and assumed to be universal and thus without ethnicity, with a frisson of novel exoticism without the potential discomfort of racist or imperialist cultural appropriation. As Ben Pitcher argues: "the [White British] consumption of Nordic culture is shaped by ideas about the relationship between geography and culture, fulfilling a desire for an 'ethnically appropriate' white culture by mapping the cultural coordinates of whiteness" (2014: 63–64). *Ragnarok*'s Whiteness is both a feature and a bug, in which White ethnicity is bifurcated into heroes and villains. The sympathetic working-class Thor-avatar Magne is affiliated with innocence, nature, and youth, which displaces Whiteness's sinister side onto the wealthy, industrialist antagonists.

The series caricatures the evil Jutuls, heaping disdain on their luxurious lifestyle: markers of this include a preposterous *dragestil*[19] mansion resembling a traditional Norwegian stave church, luxury cars, and ostentatiously branded fashions. Magne's family, in contrast, live very modestly on his mother's secretarial salary, in her late parents' distinctly well-worn house. Considering that Norway's overall wealth has increased mightily since the birth of its petroleum industry in the 1970s, and its income gaps have widened over the past twenty years in particular (Bevanger 2020), *Ragnarok*'s class politics invite speculation about Norwegian suspicion and disavowal of the very rich, as well as ambivalence about national (oil) wealth relative to the rest of the world. Thus, while the series foregrounds environmental issues, it also directs attention to the culpability of the wealthy in profiting from environmental destruction and exacerbating the climate crisis, casting the working classes as relatively innocent opponents to, and victims of, their machinations. To what extent this guilt-versus-innocence dynamic around Norwegian oil wealth can be credibly extended to a global frame will drive the analysis in the next section, but here it illuminates how even this show's small-town Norwegian setting constitutes a microcosm for the uneven distribution of wealth and risk in the Anthropocene.

Ragnarok's commitment to the conflict between good and evil characters, all but one of whom are portrayed by White actors, encourages viewers to root for Magne and his struggle to save Norwegian nature while reviling the unscrupulous Jutuls. The series thus manifests Norwegian Whiteness in divergent extradiegetic associations: Norway as an idyllic Nordic country with majestic fjords and mountains on the one hand, and, on the other, as the cultural source for historical and ongoing appropriation of Norse myth by (mostly foreign) White

---

[19] A nineteenth-century Norwegian architectural style associated with Romantic nationalism. ("Dragestil" (2023). *Store norske leksikon*. https://snl.no/dragestil.)

supremacist and neo-Nazi ideologies (see Figure 6). My analysis here is not suggesting that the show fosters White supremacy, or that it consciously manipulates this dichotomy to valorize particular forms of Whiteness. Rather, I place the series in a broader media-historical context over the past century to postulate how non-Norwegian audiences associate the country with Whiteness and, from there, to theorize how a racialized climate unconscious colors audiences' reception of *Ragnarok*'s imagined Norway.

The ambivalences inherent in mediated Norwegian Whiteness as export have a legacy that deserves more unpacking than I can do here, dating back at least to the 1930s–'40s Hollywood career of Sonja Henie. The Norwegian ice-skater-turned-actor was well known for the fact that a "fetish for material whiteness was a celebrated feature of her persona," made manifest in her insistence on the color white for her bedroom, her car, and her outfits (Negra 2001: 88). Skating fans can thank her for changing leather ice skates from black to white; less salubriously, there were reports of her fondness for and acquaintance with Adolf Hitler (Jacobs 2014). Nazi enthusiasm for the concepts of "Nordic" superiority positioned Norway at the pinnacle of White perfection, as historian Despina Stratigakos documents in her study *Hitler's Northern Utopia*: "Hitler's vision of a Germanic empire that would unite all of Europe under the rule of a superior Germanic race depended on a mystical faith in the power of Nordic blood." She explains how, drawing on the "racial science" of eugenics, a 1920s German bestseller trumpeted "the genetic superiority and nobility of the Nordic race" and "ascribed to the Nordic man a sense of adventurousness, truthfulness, and justice; a strong feeling for landscape," and many other positive attributes (Stratigakos 2020: 14–15). Today's global audiences may not have detailed knowledge of these historical associations among Norwegian Whiteness and German National Socialism, yet even clichéd portrayals of Nazis in popular media likely suffice to make the connection.

In the twenty-first century, Norwegian Whiteness again made global headlines as White supremacist mass murderer Anders Behring Breivik drew media attention to a simmering racist and xenophobic global online culture vilifying immigration and so-called "cultural Marxism," aspects of which were also ascribed to Norway's right-wing Fremskrittspartiet or Progress Party (FrP). Following Breivik's massacre of seventy-seven people on July 22, 2011, Norway saw an outpouring of national grief that included calls for openness and tolerance. This widespread public hope for a more multicultural Norway constituted "a notable shift, not least because it is an implicit recognition that dominant Norwegian society had previously not included all Norwegians" (Muller Myrdahl 2014: 488). Experts trace Breivik's international impact on other White supremacist terrorists, including in New Zealand and the United

States, perpetuating discursive links between White Nordic identity and racism (Seierstad 2019). Mediated notions of Norwegian Whiteness resurfaced yet again in connection with White supremacy in 2018, when racist US President Trump expressed a desire for more immigrants from Norway and fewer from what he called "shithole countries" such as Haiti, underscoring the frequent association of Norway with Whiteness and sparking outrage among Norwegians quick to disavow Trump (Libell and Porter 2018; Van Dam 2018). Apparently, for White supremacists both homegrown and around the world, "Nordic," including Norwegian, constitutes an admirable, aspirational White ethnic identity, frequently symbolized by a cultural heritage rooted in Norse mythology, winter sports, and rugged landscapes. Again, these racist associations do not so much reflect the tendencies of the Norwegian population at large; the popularity of wartime resistance to the Nazis and more recent (however imperfect) valorization of multiculturalism indicate quite the contrary. Indeed, the false equivalence between "Nordic" and White effectively erase the existence of Nordic citizens of color. Nevertheless, my analysis of *Ragnarok*'s racialized climate unconscious depends on recognizing the existence of these popular imaginations of Nordic Whiteness.

Ragnarok avoids playing into far-right appropriations of Nordic culture common to White supremacists from Nazi Germany to contemporary North American separatist militias, instead deploying Norse lore in service of what Scandinavian studies scholar Anna Mrozewicz terms a national "eco-exceptionalism" (2020: 85) that both exposes and represses environmental crimes and mobilizes the teenaged avatar of Thor to save Norwegian nature. As Gates has argued about race in US cinema, aesthetics and politics can be difficult to tease apart and usually reward attempts to read them as co-constitutive (2017: 44). *Ragnarok* visually evokes Norwegian Whiteness as a signifier of ethnic identity in overlapping registers through the prevalence of snowy landscapes and the Whiteness of its cast. Mrozewicz's notion of "white ecology" aptly describes this constellation of aesthetics and politics in Norwegian screen culture, dating back to World War II occupation dramas and polar-explorer films: "white ecology combines the green-ecological idealization of nature ... with the Norwegian national discourse originating in the romantic perception of (a specific type of) nature as something exceptionally Norwegian" (2020: 92; see also Waade 2017). Like Sonja Henie's penchant for the color white, the visual whiteness of national nature – snowy mountains, ice-blue fjords, glaciers – surrounding *Ragnarok*'s fictional town of Edda (named for two foundational texts in the study of Old Norse) aesthetically reinforces the aura of ethnic Whiteness already accrued around the show's central inspiration: Norse mythology and Norwegian cultural heritage. The climate unconscious of

Ragnarok's sublime landscapes threatened by climate change combines with already-existing fraught connotations associated with a Norwegian White ethnic identity to dramatize the stormy weather of Magne. In this series, the drama emanates from the way his own emotional turmoil is manifested in extreme weather, provoked by his environmentalist outrage as well as more ordinary instances of cis-male teen drama as he confronts the villains against the backdrop of Norwegian White ecology.

Weather control in *Ragnarok* symbolizes an assertion of agency by the youths and working-class residents against ancient villains. Magne's power to summon thunderstorms emerges only when he experiences extreme grief or anger, effectively converting White male feelings into weaponized weather. Whereas the threats of climate change and pollution map onto the wealthy Jutuls, the heroic White teen with learning difficulties, Magne, builds a superficially diverse coalition. A textbook example of Warner's "plastic representation" (2017) and called out by Norwegian critics as a cynical attempt to replicate the success of the more nuanced diversity of the hit teen drama *Skam* (2015–17), *Ragnarok*'s cast is populated by (late) lesbian eco-activist Isolde, queer half-sibling/Loki-incarnation Laurits, and Sri Lankan–Norwegian Freyja-avatar Iman (Danu Sunth), whose character is barely developed and whose ethnicity lacks any context. Ticking "diversity" boxes, the series also obviously deploys the hot-button issue of environmentalism, although as a more integral element. Inspired by his dead lesbian friend, Magne resists ecocrime in a story about Norwegian villains *and* Norwegian victims and heroes.

In her analysis of ecocrime in an earlier Norwegian cli-fi series that I discuss in the next section (*Occupied*), Linda Haverty Rugg detects an oscillating signification system that identifies Norwegianness with nature and foregrounds Norwegian innocence: "nature as victim moves so smoothly to Norway as victim, and then individual Norwegians as victims" (2017: 609). Yet, as Rugg points out, concern for the collective is important; in *Ragnarok* too, while the individual character conflicts play out between team Magne and team Jutul, the show spotlights environmental crime and demonstrates how it affects the townspeople (a ban on drinking the polluted tap water) and the planet (the glacier's retreat). Although Magne still hasn't prevailed over the Jutuls or successfully mastered his powers by the end of the second season, the series implies that his weather-controlling abilities will be more than a metaphor in his fight against ecocrime; the ultimate battle referenced in the series title has yet to take place, but it will likely be a fight to preserve Norway's national heritage as embodied in the mountains and fjords under threat from pollution and climate crisis. Aligning the average townspeople, including Magne's working-class family, as victims of the wealthy, immortal Jutul family, the series also models a way for Norwegians to claim agency in preserving national nature and rejecting the extraction economy that has enriched them over the past half-century. Yet situating this binary good-versus-evil struggle on Norwegian soil also fails to consider the polluting global industry that has the single biggest impact on climate change worldwide: oil. *Ragnarok* avoids examining how petroleum is the Norwegian "family business" (more aligned with the Jutuls than with Magne and friends) that bankrolls the generosity of this small, prosperous welfare state.

3.3 The Storms of Youth

This section theorizes some possibilities for cli-fi through its comparative reading of two case studies that revolve around race and ethnicity – Blackness and Whiteness – both featuring young protagonists whose ability to affect the weather appears as the only hope in a struggle against climate change. *Fast Color* exemplifies a rare Black American cli-fi narrative, with a young woman's powers figured as a potential solution to climate crisis, while *Ragnarok* deploys racialized White male Nordic identity at the center of a teen drama. Both constitute critiques of the earlier mainstream cli-fi that reduced saving the world to rescuing one's own immediate family members. Whereas first-generation cli-fi screen texts garnered apt critiques of their conformity to White heteronormative US conventions, including reproductive futurism centering on the hero father, cli-fi 2.0 brings more diverse casts and extends settings beyond the United States. By representing assertive young heroes whose wider circles of care include multiple generations and racial identities, these screen texts push the boundaries of cli-fi in their mediations of possible futures, while rebuffing the clichés of prior conventions.

Fast Color and *Ragnarok* showcase the stormy emotions that manifest as weather for young protagonists as they discover their agency in the collective pursuit of better futures. In the context of unprecedented, highly mediated global youth climate activism, cohering around the teen celebrity of Greta Thunberg, reading the climate unconscious in these texts demonstrates how they play upon viewers' existing cultural knowledge of the global Fridays for Future movement, for example. Youthful extremes of emotion in both texts activate the protagonists' weather-controlling powers, aligning neatly with Thunberg's and other young activists' assertions of rage, as expressed in Thunberg's 2019 speech at the United Nations. As a generational conflict in which the young excoriate their elders to behave responsibly, Fridays for Future shows that young people are not mere victims of climate anxiety, but capable, passionate political actors; *Fast Color* and *Ragnarok* underscore this point through their youthful protagonists, whose stormy emotions turn them into rainmakers.

4 Whiteout: Petroguilt in Norwegian Television

The Age of the Anthropocene and the array of swift social and techno-economic changes mean that the Nordic home cannot survive in a cocoon of its own goodness; it has to renew itself in more dramatic ways than it has done so far.

Nina Witoszek and Atle Midttun[20]

[T]here is something at stake in looking at, or continuing to ignore, white racial imagery. As long as race is something only applied to non-white peoples, as long as white people are not racially seen and named, they/we function as a human norm.

Richard Dyer[21]

An award-winning new design for the Norwegian passport debuted in October 2020 (see Figure 7). Its sleek, clean lines bear the hallmarks of the internationally popular Nordic aesthetic: modern, sans-serif fonts and stylized images of the forests and fjords of Norway. It even features, for added security, a black-light-activated iridescent effect that resembles the Northern Lights. This design literally inscribes images of nature into Norway's official citizenship document, foregrounding its prominence in widely held notions of national identity. According to the creators at Oslo-based Neue Design Studio's website,

The landscapes surrounding us give a sense of belonging and pride and fill a symbolic function for the entire nation. Images of scenery and landscape can easily become clichés, but by being widely accepted and deeply rooted in Norwegian culture, they are also very easy to identify with. In addition, to Norwegians, nature is more than beautiful scenery. It supplies us with rich fisheries, clean hydroelectric power, and various other industries.[22]

This explanatory text is telling precisely because it illuminates two things: the desire to appeal to an imagined Norwegian identity through the design, and the explanation about aesthetic choices and what to include or omit. The text alludes to the layered absences in the design itself: the images printed in the passport omit any industrial scenes whatsoever (as far as I can tell; I have not yet got my hands on one). Moreover, the design statement spells out the cultural knowledge that Norwegians can presumably supply on their own: that the country's wealth and welfare owe much to its efficient exploitation of natural resources, a source of national pride. Yet the text mentions only the more

---

[20] Witoszek and Midttun (2018: 13).　[21] Dyer (1997: 13).
[22] Neue Design Studio website: https://neue.no/work/norwegian-passports/.

(a)

(b)

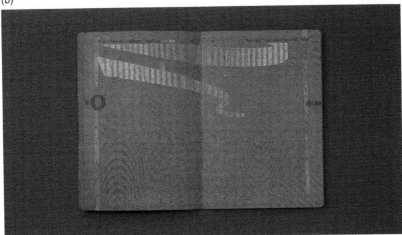

Figure 7 The design for the latest version of the Norwegian passport, by Oslo design firm Neue Design Studio, features landscapes from around the country, with a security feature that reveals the aurora borealis when illuminated by a black light

Photo: Catharina Caprino/Neue Design Studio

appealing-sounding examples, "rich fisheries, clean hydroelectric power, and various other industries," leaving out Norway's biggest industry, oil.

I open Section 4 with this official citizenship document because it serves as the baldest example of how the petroleum industry is the elephant in the room in Norwegian popular national iconography, in which nature emblematizes a national home. The "greenwashed" overtones of Neue's design and the accompanying statement echo throughout many contemporary mediations of Norwegian nature, enabling the impression that continued and expanded resource exploitation – oil and gas exploration, deep-sea mining, wind and salmon farming, and so on – will have little or no impact on the precious ecosystems that underpin the pleasures of *friluftsliv* (outdoor life). The aestheticization of nature and the enjoyment of it, evident in the national mania for skiing, hiking, and "cabin porn" (Jørgensen 2015) occupy a central place in Norway's national imaginary, so it is unsurprising that nature is frequently mobilized in the form of fjord and mountain landscapes, but in ways that do not call attention to the national reliance on extractivist industries.

Although such landscapes may appear to be a timeless representation of Norwegian nature, they are highly mediated and aestheticized, doing a lot of work for notions of national identity; as Barbara Bender aptly point out, "the engagement with landscape and time is historically particular, imbricated in social relations and deeply political" (Bender 2002: 104; see also Saunders 2020). As Anna Mrozewicz's provocative notion of "white ecology" implies, Norwegian screen culture has long relied on associations among nation, nature, and Whiteness, and more specifically between the "white frozen landscape" and White Norwegian innocence (2020: 94), associations that pertain to *Ragnarok* in Section 3 as well as the case studies that follow. The climate unconscious offers a way to unpack how twenty-first-century Norwegian television series negotiate these palimpsestic meanings (or avoid doing so), particularly in relation to the presence or absence of oil in the picture. In the Norwegian context, Nina Witoszek and Atle Midttun remind us, "the emergent, electrifying narrative of success – combined with prosperity and unspoiled beauty of nature – has been so potent that even the country's high, oil-lubricated ecological footprint has been eclipsed by upbeat 'green stories'" (2018: 3). Often Bender's social and political contexts are not immediately visible, due to the eclipse of oil in the landscapes described here, and for this reason, the elision of traces of industry in such pristine landscapes bears closer scrutiny (see Figure 7).

These image regimes exemplify what Nicholas Mirzoeff calls Anthropocene visuality, which "allows us to move on, to see nothing and keep circulating commodities, despite the destruction of the biosphere" (2014: 217; see also Vik 2017). This "nothing-to-see-here" mode of visuality permeates the Norwegian imagination of national nature, celebrated not only in the new passport but in innumerable images of sublime landscapes nestled alongside messaging about the progressive environmental policies commonly ascribed to the Nordic countries. The paradoxes inherent in this "green," natural image, when seen in light of Norway's reliance on the fossil-fuel industries, attest to the fact that the "greening of the Nordic countries is by no means a given process but rather a complex, potentially hypocritical form of sustainable development and resource management, involving both greenwashing and contradictory public relations as well as inspiring idealism and resourceful environmentalist activism" (Kääpä 2014: 10). Indeed, the deployment of Anthropocene visuality in Norwegian visual culture and its frequent reference to national nature along with other key features of Norwegian identity, have for decades dominated the realm of scripted television, which this section examines in more detail to identify the avoidance strategies that have kept oil out of the picture heretofore.

With the release of three series over a period of three years, *Okkupert* [*Occupied*] (2015–, TV2), *Lykkeland* [*State of Happiness*] (2018–, NRK), and *Oljefondet* [*The Oil Fund*] (2018–, TVNorge), Norwegian screen culture experienced a belated oil boom, coming about fifty years after the discovery of oil in Norwegian waters.[23] While there probably has not been any overt effort to keep the oil industry off the screen, it struck me as a glaring absence when I moved here in 2017, given that one of the first things I learned about my new home was the dramatic economic impact of the oil industry, originating in the year I was born, 1969. Why, then, have there been so few fiction films or television series that portray the Norwegian oil industry, even as a backdrop, until this century? Aside from the 1990s primetime soap *Offshore* and the 2013 conspiracy thriller film *Pionér* (*Pioneer*), this sea change in Norwegian history has remained invisible in screen fictions. As I and my coauthors argue in an article about climate change in Norwegian literature, film, and television, "oil remained an absent signifier through much of the twentieth century" (Furuseth et al. 2020: 13). Newspaper commentator Andreas Økland noted this belated attention to oil in Norwegian screen storytelling upon the release of *State of Happiness*, in a review entitled "Norge trenger et series som *Lykkeland*" ("Norway needs a series like *State of Happiness*") in which he writes, "Den fyller det som framstår som et gapende tomrom i norsk populærkultur" ("It fills what seems to be a gaping hole in Norwegian popular culture") (Økland 2018: n.p., my translation). Indeed, this lacuna and its very recent exceptions pushed me to further investigate ways to study Norwegian screen petrocultures, inquiring into the few instances of oil thematics on screen and at the same time, as in the passport design, uncovering traces of its occlusion and greenwashing.

I argue that this long screen silence is itself an instance of the climate unconscious at work, operating in the context of what sociologist Kari

---

[23] The Norwegian oil-field disaster film *Nordsjøen* (*The Burning Sea*) (2021) promises rich material for future analysis. The film centers on a White female engineer rescuing her romantic partner from certain death (devoting much screen time to his adorable son) and provides product placement for a real-life Norwegian deep-sea robotics technology company.

Norgaard describes as the "normalizing narratives" that help Norwegians maintain a positive national identity (2011: 11). The confident self-regard fostered by oil-enabled prosperity and the social-democratic welfare state can be identified in the findings that "the majority of Norway's citizens are convinced that they have reached – at least in the current moment of history – a *eudaemonic condition*: the apex of human flourishing and happiness on earth" (Witoszek and Midttun 2018: 14). Norgaard points out that the good life in Norwegian (and, more broadly, Western) society during the latter third of the twentieth century required negotiating a path between knowing the facts about climate change and neglecting "to integrate this knowledge into everyday life or to transform it into social action" (2011: 11). While a minority resort to overt denial, most pick their way through a thicket of emotional avoidance strategies that Norgaard categorizes collectively as a "social organization of denial," which enables them to sidestep the discomfort that might accompany a full and honest reckoning with climate realities, including facing up to Norway's complicity as a leader in the fossil-fuel industries (12). In this context of avoidance, overt, realistic representations of climate change and things now directly associated with it – extreme weather, fossil-fuel industries – can be held at arm's length.

Interrogating the handful of recent exceptions in which oil is overtly thematized, as well as the unwritten rule that oil remain unrepresented for most of the last half-century, this section takes up the other temporal phenomenon that characterizes Norwegian screen petrocultures – allusions to and mediations of the past – as well as the complex affective scenarios, at the heart of particular genres such as the political thriller and the melodrama, that threaten to reduce environmental issues to backdrops or plot devices rather than centering them and subjecting them to stronger scrutiny. The fact that these scripted series are among the first to break with the climate unconscious and directly focus on the Norwegian oil business demands further scholarly attention, starting with the always useful and provocative questions central to cultural studies scholarship: why this text now? What does it say to us about the time and place in which it was produced and released? What might the aesthetic choices on display in the series further illuminate when placed in an explicitly petrocultural context? After outlining a petrocultural approach suited to a Norwegian context, this section analyzes two recent series focusing on the interplay between their affective ecologies (marked by guilt, patriotism, religious feeling) and their televisual form's complex engagements with Norway's pasts and presents. This analysis of Norwegian screen fiction's oil narratives reveals how reading for the climate unconscious can account for oil's presences and absences in this privileged, majority-White society.

4.1 Petrocultures, Norwegian Style

Taking up these recent oil-focused series, however, makes it clear that the study of Norwegian petrocultures must also theorize the sudden appearance of oil narratives; such investigations thus also afford a window onto the myriad hidden, or repressed, traces of its petrocultures in the previous decades for future research. The groundbreaking work of North American petroculture studies provides a point of departure, drawing connections between oil culture and notions of Americanness. Daniel Worden's notion of "fossil-fuel futurity" conveys his observation, demonstrated in close readings of the serialized novel and film adaptation *Giant* (1956) alongside the TV series *Dallas* (1978–91) and the film *There Will Be Blood* (2007), that "[i]t is difficult to imagine a future without petroleum, in part because petroleum underlies the normative vision of family, work, and social belonging in the late twentieth-century United States" (Worden 2012: 441). In his study of oil and automobility, geographer Matthew Huber points out that, in the United States, "[o]il is a powerful force not only because of the material geographies of mobility it makes possible but also because its combustion often accompanies deeply felt visions of freedom and individualism" (2013: xi; see also Leyda 2016a: 129–137). The embeddedness of hydrocarbon-based energy in the spatialities of everyday life shapes contemporary attitudes toward politics and "the good life," broadly construed, in that Americans and many others in developed countries have been able, for the most part, to take for granted the stability of the energy supply that undergirds the functioning of social relations (Wenzel 2017: 11).

Huber's work and that of other scholars of oil culture document how the pursuit of perceived positives such as freedom and prosperity can make it difficult to face the damage that extraction industries inflict on the good life, as in the case of pollution, anthropogenic climate change, and fracking earthquakes. On the other hand, the sunny American values of freedom and individualism that scholarship on automobility often cites can also take on a darker aspect. In her work on masculinity and petroculture, political scientist Cara Daggett investigates "fuel fascism," a Trump-era emergent political formation located at a moment of "convergence ... between climate change, a threated fossil fuel system, and an increasingly fragile Western hypermasculinity" (2018: 27–29). Petromasculinity indicates that the sense of entitlement to the "good life" that Americans have historically come to expect, including a high standard of living built around automobility (which grants access to personal privacy, mobility, and freedom), derives from fossil fuels, which thus form the basis for the social relations and spatialities associated with an American way of life currently and increasingly under threat.

My reading strategy highlighting the climate unconscious dovetails here with a petrocultures approach when taken to its logical conclusion. Moving beyond the thematics of oil and the automobile, petroculture studies today works from the premise that, in fact, all culture produced in the age of oil bears some traces of its provenance. In addition to calling attention to details such as the presence of energy sources and energy consumption in a text, which can be foregrounded to examine taken-for-granted assumptions about the cultural values that underlie all art works, research in energy humanities pushes scholars to consider approaches that place energy sources at the center of their analytical frameworks such as periodization. Imre Szeman points out that "[e]xtraction needs to be a part of any and every account of our neoliberal present and of the politics required to address its inequalities and injustices" (2017: 445). Further, as Jennifer Wenzel (2017) asserts, the absences and silences in cultural productions also speak loudly to those prepared to hear:

> energy has been the great not-said (or, in terms of reception, not-seen, unread) in cultural production during the unprecedented and unrepeatable moment of abundant cheap energy in the past century or more. This is the great paradox of fossil fuel imaginaries: in literature as in life, oil in particular is at once everywhere and nowhere, indispensable yet largely unapprehended, not so much invisible as unseen. (2017: 11)

As demonstrated in my analysis of the Norwegian passport design at the beginning of Section 4, Wenzel's gambit broaches new possibilities for petrocultures research by suggesting that this work is not only interpretive but archaeological, uncovering the way oil imaginaries may have been buried or erased (see Figure 7). Wenzel pushes past what she calls the "hook of the thematic" in search of more complex aesthetic considerations: "Beyond questions of theme, how else do genre and other matters of form look different when we consider energy? What work do particular cultural forms do in making our relation to energy visible or obscuring it from view?" (2017: 11; 13).

While these questions of genre and form ground my work on the affects of Norwegian petrocultures and their embeddedness in the temporalities of the past, the fact that the petrocultures field has been built largely around North American material and scholarly milieux necessitates a theoretical bridge in order for it to work in a Norwegian context, where the sense of national identity and its relation to oil is quite different. Indeed, research on other regions such as the Niger Delta (Okuyade 2011), Latin America (Acker 2020), and the North Sea (Ritson 2019) also beckons, with the promise of accordingly varied cultural contexts. This section extends the study of petrocultures to Norway, "a privileged periphery," where a longstanding identification with nature as the source of the country's natural resources, from fisheries and timber to petroleum, has fueled its economy for centuries (Thue 2008: 394; see also Cleary 2016). As in the designs for the new Norwegian passport, northern landscape iconography frequently operates as a shorthand for an idealized national identity; in screen representations, these landscapes also often fold in other common perceptions of wealthy, social-democratic Norway as both green (in environmental policy) and White (in demographics) (see Figure 7). Contemporary television here participates in Norgaard's socially organized denial, offering audiences ways to sidestep petroguilt via, for example, narratives of White innocence that manifest in *Ragnarok* as youth activism, as discussed in Section 3, and of nostalgia for pre-petroleum Norway's humble origins.

Before the discovery of oil, Norway was one of the poorer countries in Europe, as a glib *Guardian* television reviewer puts it: "[*State of Happiness*] shows how, but for oil, Norway, with its mutton farms and Jesus-love, might have taken a very different back route to the twenty-first century, almost up there with Albania" (Ferguson 2020). Thanks to careful management of the industry and its profits, however, residents of this privileged oil-rich periphery are now well-off enough to feel pangs of conscience, as Witoszek and Midttun write: "having obtained most things they desired, [Norwegians] are now more aware of the colossal gap between their affluence and the genuine need and misery in other parts of the world" (2018: 14). Where the US study of petro-cultures must take into account the cultural valorization of individualism, freedom, and mobility that oil signifies in that national imaginary, and which, taken to extremes, finds expression in petromasculinity and fuel fascism, the Norwegian case could not be more different.

The concept of "sustainable modernity" characterizes the Scandinavian region, emphasizing close relations with nature and a prosocial "domestica-tion" of the state as familial, similar to the Swedish idea of the *folkhemmet* (people's home): "the myth of the state as a fatherly protector of individual autonomy, and the perception of society as a 'family,' constitute a strong legacy, which tempers modernity's uprooting and disinheriting thrust" (Witoszek and Midttun 2018: 13). The Norwegian self-conception of the nation as family, and an affluent one at that, shapes the way the national imagination relates to oil; it also makes the domestic melodrama an apt choice for the historical television series about the early impacts of oil on Norway, *State of Happiness*. The series's all-White ensemble cast provides a microcosm of late 1960s Norway: working-class farmers and fishers, devout Christians, ambitious youth, go-getter local politicians, and melancholy patri-cian housewives provide today's audiences with sympathetic figures of their national past, poised to experience momentous change.

In some ways analogous to the fictional country of Wakanda in *Black Panther*, wealthy and prosperous thanks to the extraction of vibranium (explored in Section 2.2), Norway is widely noted as an exceptional petrostate in that it has avoided the pitfalls of the "resource curse" by establishing a relatively transparent national oil fund and maintaining a functioning social democracy with minimal corruption or poverty. The success story of Norway's economic prosperity and relatively egalitarian social welfare state – which contributes to its position near the top of the World Happiness Report's list for many years running – also fosters the Norwegian variety of what literary scholar Elisabeth Oxfeldt terms "scanguilt," a phenomenon whereby Scandinavians recognize their privilege relative to the rest of the world, leading to experiences of guilt (2016: 10). Because of its economic reliance on the petroleum industry, as Scandinavianist Ellen Rees contends, Norway's variety of scanguilt takes the form of "petro-guilt," a largely repressed feeling that could complicate a collective sense of innocence and moral superiority; as a result, one of the country's few films about the oil industry (set abroad) "deftly avoids fully engaging with the exploitation and associated guilt that underlies its plot" (2016: 47, 44). Rees's analysis of that film, *Limbo* (2010), set in the Caribbean and featuring characters of many nationalities, unpacks the interconnectedness of race, class, and nationality in White Scandinavians' petroguilt. Her 2016 article further documents how, despite the 2009 publication of "three scathing critiques of the Norwegian oil industry," a "strategy of acting like nothing is wrong continues to dominate Norwegian public discourse" (2016: 46–47). In line with Norgaard's notion of the social organization of denial and Mirzoeff's "nothing-to-see-here" Anthropocene visuality, this avoidant strategy in Norway persists: the latest parliamentary elections highlighted the importance of *oljepolitikk* (oil policy). As recently as October 2021, the Sosialistisk Venstreparti (SV), or Socialist Left party, broke off negotiations to form a government with neoliberal center-left parties over the issue of *oljepolitikk*, joining the Green party and the Marxist party in proposing legislation to end petroleum exploration (Ummelas 2021; Elster 2021). Although public support for environmentalist policy is steadily growing in Norway, the prevailing avoidance strategy continues to steer the ship of state when it comes to the oil industry.

In my investigation of the long scarcity and recent surfacing of oil on Norwegian popular television, I employ Rees's concept of petroguilt to express the regionally specific affective dimensions of petrocultures. Just as "petromelancholia" refers to "the grieving of conventional oil resources and the pleasures they sustained" in the developed world (LeMenager 2014: 102) and "solastalgia" demarcates the pain experienced at the loss of one's homeplace to environmental damage (Albrecht et al. 2007: S96), both of which increasingly find expression in Norwegian screen culture as well, petroguilt describes a specifically Norwegian affect that exists in tension with other facets of Norwegian national identity, articulating "moral discomfort, accompanied by concerns about climate change and environmental crisis" (Witoszek and Midttun 2018: 14). The case studies that close out this section draw together some of these productive lines of inquiry to theorize Norwegian screen petro-cultures in two ways: first, by examining the deployment of ambivalent affects in the respective genres of melodrama and thriller, each with references to Norwegian pasts and to "domestic" contexts in both senses of the word, and then by zooming in on televisual aesthetics and the particular affordances of the serial form, ensemble casts, and the "complexity" that brands the prestige drama format.

4.2 Nostalgia and the Avoidance of Petroguilt in *State of Happiness*

The historical drama *State of Happiness* and the political thriller *Occupied* both articulate, in quite different registers, the affective investments surrounding Norwegian petroculture that are only now emerging into popular screen representations. These affects are divergent: an ambience of cozy familiarity and nostalgia suffuses *State*'s national mythmaking around the origin story of Norway's oil encounter, while a prevailing sense of dread and suspense drives *Occupied*'s near-future, far-fetched parable about a Russian occupation of Norway's oil industry. However, reading them together for the operation of the climate unconscious reveals the same affective engine powering both series: petroguilt and its intimate imbrications in Norwegian pasts. The prevailing Whiteness of both series' central figures also demonstrates the relative paucity of screen diversity in Norway to date, and the ongoing availability of Norwegian quality television for viewing audiences abroad seeking what Pitcher dubs "ethnically appropriate" Nordic exoticism, as discussed in connection with *Ragnarok* in Section 3.2 (2014: 63–64).

Family and romantic conflicts in both series provide compelling plotlines to balance out their industrial and political plotlines, blending public and private spheres and introducing domestic settings as an integral part of the drama. These story elements, which in *State of Happiness* prompt some critics to invoke the soap-opera genre with varying degrees of condescension (Rowat 2020), nevertheless demonstrate how petroleum can run "ultradeep" in cultural narratives, in terms of what LeMenager describes as the "relationship between we moderns and oil" (LeMenager 2014: 6–13). Feminist cultural studies scholars have demonstrated that soaps can be valuable in television studies and popular culture studies, as Ien Ang's (2013; first published in 1992) landmark scholarship on the US oil melodrama *Dallas* (1985) has shown (also interestingly an indication of how oil-saturated US television culture is relative to Norway). *State* focalizes the emotional as well as economic consequences of the oil boom years, which means toggling between a micro and macro viewpoint, humanizing the individuals affected by the industry fifty years ago, and encouraging contemporary viewers to identify with them, across the temporal divide, at that pivotal moment in Norwegian history before petroguilt grew into a (repressed) cultural dominant.

Thanks to the extended running time of the television drama format (eight one-hour episodes in the first season), *State of Happiness* can unfold multiple storylines that take on the myriad impacts of the oil industry on Norway's people and institutions. The series is valuable in the study of Norwegian petrocultures because it exemplifies the extent to which the historical melodrama's unavoidable presentism, combined with its narrative complexity, can operate as a climate unconscious that heightens the dramatic irony arising from the disconnect between, on the one hand, today's eco-ethics and petropolitics, and the undiluted excitement that met most of the early days of the oil boom, on the other. Like any historical fiction, *State* navigates the twin shoals of presentism and nostalgia as it strives to build and maintain viewer engagement with characters of a different era. This big-budget production constructs an attractive myth around (White) Norwegian national identity at that major transitional moment, inviting viewers to relate to comparatively naïve attitudes toward the oil industry.

Deciding how to construct the origin story of Norwegian oil for contemporary audiences meant devising a nationally meaningful historical drama that appeals to audiences watching during the declining years of petromodernity, when its best years are already behind us. Series writer Mette Bølstad acknowledges as much as she explains her process:

> It's easy to have a negative spin on everything, a kind of ironic distance with past events. But we need the patience to live with the people in the time, without this kind of negative hindsight. . . . It was crucial in the first season to get close to the characters, . . . That's when you can keep the idealistic point of view and capture the euphoria of the time. (Pham 2018: n.p.)

Asked about the risk of fostering a strain of smug presentism among today's climate-crisis-aware viewers, Bølstad admits that she consciously avoided "those scenes where we have the perspective of 'now' talking about 'then.' This is not a Philip Morris story, this is not big tobacco. So it's important to keep that. My generation did know a bit. There were a lot of marches against pollution in my generation. But we didn't know exactly about oil" (Dowell 2020). This assertion of generational innocence is built into the series, in which Norwegians are excited about the discovery of oil as a source of economic growth, employment, and, for some, personal wealth, and none express reservations about the future environmental impact of the industry on Norway or the rest of the world.

The affective power of the melodramatic form allows the series to draw in contemporary audiences, to convey not so much the factual history of oil's discovery, but its emotional impact for Norwegians in 1969. In one particularly rich sequence at the end of Episode 2, "Røykforbud [Smoking ban]," *State of Happiness* conveys the affective punch of the moment with not only exuberance, but a hint of Christian reverence (see Figure 8). The series establishes the importance of devout Protestantism in Stavanger, at the heart of Norway's southern "Bible belt," as a complex religious community that both supports and disciplines its members. The episode's closing montage depicts the fateful December night when the oil platform lights up with burn-off, signaling a major discovery; the visually dazzling montage of the crew gazing in wonder at the flames is set to the popular nineteenth-century church hymn "Deilig er Jorden," widely sung at Christmastime as well as funerals.[24] The choice of music for this montage thus directly parallels the discovery of oil with the coming of the Christian savior who will lead believers to paradise.[25] The unvarnished joy

---

[24] This sequence reinforces a widely held belief that oil was discovered just before Christmas; yet, as Cleary points out, "in fact the find was made in September, and then after evaluating the results, a senior executive at Phillips telephoned the minister of industry on 23 December and told him, 'I think we have an oilfield'" (2016: 27).

[25] The song was a popular German hymn, translated into Danish and Norwegian. English versions have titles like "Fairest Lord Jesus" or "Beautiful Savior," but the Norwegian title, and its first line, means literally "the earth is lovely." Lyrics in Norwegian followed by my literal translation.

Deilig er jorden,	Lovely is the Earth,
prektig er guds himmel,	mighty is God's heaven,
skjønn er sjelenes pilgrimsgang!	beautiful are the souls' pilgrimages!
Gjennom de fagre	Through the beautiful
riker på jorden	kingdoms of the Earth
går vi til paradis med sang.	we walk singing to paradise.
Tider skal komme,	Ages will come,
tider skal henrulle,	ages will pass,
slekt skal følge slekters gang,	kin will follow kin,
aldri forstummer	never will cease
tonen fra himlen	the tones from heaven
i sjelens glade pilgrimssang.	in the soul's joyful pilgrim-song.
Englene sang den	The angels sang it
først for markens hyrder;	first for the shepherds of the field;
skjønt fra sjel til sjel det lød:	from soul to soul it sounded:
fred over jorden,	peace on earth,
menneske, fryd deg!	people, rejoice!
Oss er en evig frelser født!	To us an eternal savior is born!

Figure 8 *State of Happiness* (2018–) portrays the discovery of Norwegian oil in December 1969 in a montage sequence that include numerous shots of oil–rig workers bathed in golden light, with halo-like effects, as a popular Christian hymn about the beautiful Earth as a blessing from God accompanies the scene (S1E2 "Smoking Ban").

among the characters in this scene is moving, despite what audiences today know about the effects of oil and other fossil fuels on the biosphere. This contemporary awareness is heightened by the music: genuine delight in this "salvation" is tempered by viewers' knowledge of oil's mixed blessings for the "beautiful" Earth. Yet the golden halos, caused by lens flares, encircling the heads of the rig workers, mark their innocence as blessedness at that major turning point in Norwegian history. Their state of happiness, visible in their faces and under-scored visually by the lighting's effects, shows them (and Norway more gener-ally) as grateful recipients of God's blessings on Earth (*jorden*) thanks to their access to the resources under the ocean floor, the ultimate Christmas gift.

The emotion portrayed in the montage, alluding to the Christian religious experience of salvation in which many in 1960s Norway believed, also serves to remind contemporary audiences of the temporal distance of fifty-odd years (see Figure 8). Indeed, it is impossible to view *State of Happiness* without sensing the dramatic irony that complicates its presentism; viewers today recognize the significance of its petronarrative in light of contemporary national and global struggles over ecological ethics. By putting audiences in the shoes of ordinary Norwegians at the time who saw only the gains to come, and who did not yet realize the negative consequences of oil extraction, the narrative straddles the divide that separates them from today's advantage of hindsight and allows viewers to indulge in a vicarious innocence now foreclosed. The moment when the Norwegian *oljeeventyr*, which translates as either oil fairy-tale or oil adventure, begins also marks the moment when Norgaard's strategies of social avoidance of petroguilt begin to gestate. By celebrating that purportedly guiltless original moment in late 1969, *State* promises to document the decades of Norway's oil encounter: Season 1 portrays 1969–72, while Season 2 covers 1977–80, including a 1977 uncontrolled blowout and the 1980 Alexander L. Kielland oil-platform disaster in which 123 people died. The series thus dramatizes Norway's ongoing national negotiations with, and disavowals of, petroguilt by portraying the innocence and euphoria of discovery; at the same time, via the climate unconscious inherent in the temporal gap between the show's historical setting and its reception, viewers are also already aware of the subsequent costs.

The operation of such temporalities in the reception of historical dramas involves a delicate balance of affect and aesthetics. Reviews of *State of Happiness* frequently draw comparisons with the hit US quality television series *Mad Men* (2007–15), with its seductive 1960s aesthetic and shockingly outdated social mores (Dowell 2020). Notably, in its genre of historical melodrama revolving around a male-dominated industry, *State* (like *Mad Men* before it) also manages to include women's experiences. With a broad (all-White) ensemble cast, this series zooms out to portray a wider swathe of the nascent oil culture as it impacts not only business and politics but also private life, including women's roles in the office and the family, the role of the church in the community, and the effects of class mobility. Also like *Mad Men*, this series tiptoes through the minefields of nostalgia and presentism, allowing for the visual pleasure of a high-budget, lushly designed prestige TV series while (for the most part) eschewing, on the one hand, full-throated defenses of the earlier era's now-obvious blind spots or, on the other, condescending dismissals of those benighted characters who did not know then what we know now. As film scholar Dana Polan points out, the anti-hero protagonist of *Mad Men*, Don Draper, is constantly "on the wrong side of history," supporting Richard Nixon, betting against Cassius Clay, and hating the Beatles. Polan's assessment also rings true for *State of Happiness*:

> *Mad Men* needs from us this recognition of the characters' fallibility in history because it is key to the way we watch the show from our historical present and reflect back on fraught lives such as Don's and the mistakes he (and others around him) often make as they grope toward a new world for which they are only partially prepared. (2013: 43)

Watching Season 1 of *State of Happiness*, viewers are uneasily aware that, in environmental terms, the oil industry is also on the wrong side of history;

indeed, the climate unconscious forms an ever-present background thrum, along with the American rock soundtrack. Interestingly, however, the Whiteness of the show's nostalgic late-1960s aesthetic also, like *Mad Men*'s, appears outdated and naïve, portraying a pre-petroguilt Norway in which White US Americans are the only foreigners. This staging of the nascent, innocent petrostate thus comes across as both visually pleasing nostalgia and as a picture of a mythical all-White past.

4.3 Negotiating Petroguilt in *Occupied*

Turning from a historical series to a speculative one set in the near future, *Occupied* taps into multiple cultural memories and geopolitical conflicts pertaining to both Norway and Russia, beginning with its title, which calls to mind the World War II German occupation of Norway between 1940 and 1945 and situates the series within the rich archive of subsequent "occupation dramas" in Norwegian cinema (Iversen and Sørenssen 1996: 191–192). *Occupied* constructs a fictional future that in fact remediates its historical and cinematic pasts through direct allusions to that popular and plentiful postwar subgenre.[26] But beyond its allusions to (mediations of) past events, *Occupied* also portrays a possible future. Media scholar Richard Grusin's concept of "premediation" offers a way to explain how this series represents its far-fetched near-future scenario of a Russian-occupied Norway. To avoid the surprise trauma of another event like 9/11 in the United States (in this series, a catastrophic hurricane in Norway and subsequent loss of sovereignty), Grusin argues, contemporary media premediate disaster before it happens, thereby both expressing and contributing to ambient anxieties about disasters (Grusin 2010: 4).

The series uncovers complacency and self-interest beneath the placid surface of Norwegian affluence, played out in an implausible geopolitical scenario. Resistance to the oil-free future decreed by Green party Prime Minister Jesper Berg (Henrik Mestad) in Season 1 comes primarily from Russia, flexing its muscles against its smaller, more prosperous neighbor in the program's updating of the tried-and-true historical formula of the occupation drama. While a future in which Russia occupies Norway strains credibility, *Occupied* does articulate a very real and growing sense of dread of the future, in which the climate crisis threatens major disruptions of everyday life and energy transition endangers Norway's lucrative oil industry.

Occupied grabbed the international media spotlight for its unapologetically provocative premise: that a sovereign state could be occupied by another solely

---

[26] See Leyda 2018. Part of my analysis of *Occupied* here draws on this article.

for the purpose of controlling its fossil-fuel resources.[27] Aside from obvious parallels with the Iraq War, the show's scenario evokes multiple narratives of geopolitical conflict, including World War II, in which Norway usually figures as innocent victim. According to Erik Skjoldbærg, one of the show's creators and directors, inspiration for the series lies in the experience of Nazi occupation, decades before the discovery of the vast fossil-fuel reserves that would make Norway rich: "When you look back at what really happened during WWII in Norway, it's easy to think that most people were in opposition but the truth is that not everyone was a hero, a lot of people did nothing, some were collaborators and some even took advantage of the situation" (Hopewell 2016: n.p.). As in *Ragnarok*, a good-versus-evil story guides viewers to root for the righteous and disavow the morally tainted. Mobilizing memories of a highly mediated history of embattled patriotism and callow treason, *Occupied* constructs a scenario in which fossil fuels lie at the center of the chain of events that leads to the invasion and occupation, tentatively linking support for sustainable energy policy with love of country (as well as planet).[28]

Occupied draws on the popular archive of cultural memory pertaining to a conflicted Norwegian resistance in which the show's ensemble cast of characters all struggle in notably different ways with conflicting personal and patriotic allegiances that come under duress. The series format, with many more hours in which to unfold its narrative, allows for a broader canvas than a feature film, situating its characters within a complicated web of loyalties and betrayals. While many of the characters, including Berg and the investigative journalist Thomas Eriksen (Vegar Hoel) are motivated by their love of country and desire to keep the peace, the series emphasizes the personal costs they incur: marital strife, familial resentment, even mortal danger. In their painful dilemmas, these characters sometimes come across as weak or indecisive as well as occasionally heroic. While Berg is accused of capitulation as Russia takes control of his country's oil industry and Eriksen ends up dead, the series positions journalist Eriksen's wife Bente Norum (Ane Dahl Torp) as the real quisling at the heart of a Norwegian family (see Figure 9). She is also most relevant to my interest in petroguilt and its role in the climate unconscious in *Occupied*.

In line with, and at times exceeding the ambivalent heroism that marked earlier iterations of the occupation drama, Bente secures her own advantage through the patronage of the (increasingly unpopular) Russians, seeing her husband's journalistic idealism as self-indulgent recklessness that puts the family's well-being at risk. Bente is headstrong and flawed; she values her

---

[27] I explore parallels with Russia's conflicts in Georgia and Ukraine in Leyda 2018.

[28] This moral distinction becomes muddier in subsequent seasons, as Mrozewicz points out (2020: 97).

Figure 9 The character of Bente (Ane Dahl Torp) in *Occupied* (2015–20),
whose restaurant caters to Russian diplomats, embodies the
ambivalences inherent in Norwegian petroguilt, often torn between profit and
patriotism

own immediate well-being over any noble devotion to the environment, or the nation and its sovereignty. Her marriage suffers from several factors, including her resentment of Thomas's lack of income as he pursues a story related to the Russian crisis, her struggling restaurant's dependence on wealthy Russian customers from the nearby embassy, and her affair with a Russian diplomat (see Figure 9). She does not hesitate to make decisions based entirely on what will benefit herself and her family, even when this means siding with the Russians, who are increasingly framed as an occupying enemy.

The complexity of *Occupied*'s engagement with national identity in the person of Bente is rooted in ambivalent recollections of World War II from the family members of its two high-profile creators. Showrunner Skjoldbærg learned about the war from his grandfather, and cocreator Jo Nesbø from his father; Nesbø's 2014 novel *The Redbreast* critiques what he terms "the mythical self-image of the Norwegian people as a nation actively resisting Hitler" (Nesbø 2014: n.p.). Recalling the collaborator figure from World War II films, Bente represents a pragmatic, ambitious person who sees within her reach a successful business and a rewarding romantic relationship. Without 'demonizing her as a one-dimensional traitor, *Occupied* portrays her apolitical egoism in a dubious light, as she not only undercuts her husband's pursuit of journalistic truth, but also refuses to altruistically support her government's attempt to make amends for its petroguilt by shutting down its fossil-fuel exports. Bente's complicated self-interest becomes legible as a wider critique through Norgaard's analysis of the social organization of denial: personifying self-centered short-sightedness, her character develops through her experience of many of the same conditions that enable Norway's disavowal of its petroguilt. Read allegorically, if Bente stands for Norwegian petroguilt made manifest, then Russia occupies the role of petroleum itself, in that Bente is seduced by and benefits directly from her relationship with it, ignoring the resulting havoc and against objections from family and friends.[29] As a not-entirely-unsympathetic character, Bente thus constitutes a challenge to the prevalent discourse of national innocence; her understandable desire for comfort, success, and stability leads her into ethical peril, yet her character's flawed humanity also makes complete disavowal difficult.

4.4 Innocence and Ambivalence in Norwegian Petrodrama

Faced with the sudden surfacing of the Norwegian oil industry in fiction film and television after such a long absence in the decades since its discovery, this section develops a theoretical framework for the analysis of two recent series. My approach to Norwegian screen petrocultures considers Norway's unique position as a petrostate with a reputation for environmentally progressive attitudes and a national identity strongly oriented around the love of nature. Weaving together relevant theories from the environmental humanities, Scandinavian studies, and screen studies, I employ the concept of petroguilt as a lens through which to view the operations of the climate unconscious in *State of Happiness* and *Occupied*. As I observed in Section 3's discussion of *Ragnarok*, these series mediate some of the ways Norwegian public discourse depends on a spectrum of socially organized denial and rhetorics of national innocence, racialized as White but treated as unmarked. In contrast to *Ragnarok*'s narrative propulsion toward a confrontation with those responsible for environmental damage, however, neither petrodrama reassures viewers that a solution is forthcoming. *Occupied* warns that hasty anti-oil policies endanger Norway's sovereignty and thus its ability to uphold its reputation as a nature-loving social welfare utopia, while *State of Happiness* indulges viewers in a nostalgic, time-shifted generational innocence by placing viewers in the shoes of their forebears, who did not realize the consequences of figuring oil as savior. Both series depend on the climate unconscious, which allows audiences to recognize the way petroguilt permeates contemporary Norwegian culture, where oil as a thematic has been unacknowledged until quite recently.

Like the national narrative articulated in *Black Panther*'s Wakanda, Norway's positive self-image depends on its successful economic and affective management of its resource blessing. However, this is petroleum, not the clean

---

[29] Many thanks to Johanna Conterio for her astute feedback on this point.

miracle substance vibranium, and thus Norway must work ever harder to preserve its exceptionalism. For several decades, this meant that Norwegian screen fiction avoided oil almost entirely, making the climate unconscious an apposite way to theorize its absence. Now, however, the mediation of Norwegian petrocultures has entered a new stage, with growing public concern about accountability and culpability threatening to break the long silence and with new series and films broaching issues long dormant. Just as *Ragnarok* and *Fast Color* attest to the power of cli-fi 2.0 to mediate youth climate activism, *State of Happiness* and *Occupied* demonstrate the currency of the ongoing negotiation of petroguilt in Norwegian prestige drama.

5 Coda

As I finalized the manuscript of this Element in early 2023, skeptical headlines were already circulating about this year's upcoming UN Climate Change Conference (COP28 in the United Arab Emirates), which would once again attempt to wring consensus from the reticent leaders who had failed since Paris (2015) to establish a workable plan to keep Earth inhabitable. Convened by the head of the UAE's state-run oil company, the conference attracted scorn from activists like Greta Thunberg, who characterized the choice of location as "ridiculous" (Wearden 2023). Throughout this study, in addition to policy boondoggles, I cite relevant reports about the extreme weather disasters that mark the Anthropocene's new normal: wildfires, hurricanes, floods, droughts, heatwaves. Doubtless these will be soon superseded; today's looping cycle of climate crisis news and the ensuing anxiety only corroborate the need for reading strategies that help make sense of the mediated structures of feeling that permeate contemporary life. And while the expanding genre of cli-fi merits further study, other screen texts that are not explicitly about climate change also make worthwhile case studies through which to observe the current climate unconscious as it punctuates most people's daily media consumption.

Anthroposcreens demonstrates that an often-unacknowledged baseline awareness of environmental crisis is always present in screen texts, churning below the surface. The relentless pace of climate reporting ensures that cultural knowledge about climate change is ever-present in most people's background processes, operating at the level of affect and form. Reading for this climate unconscious enables viewers of contemporary film and television to think through the affective affordances of genre and aesthetics, foregrounding those processes. This project argues for a reading strategy that attends to absences and presences of many kinds: in both diegetic and nondiegetic worlds, in academic disciplines and methods, in taken-for-granted and unexpected texts. Although literary ecocriticism now addresses the enduring dominance of White and US American texts and perspectives in literature and genre fiction, there is no comparable body of critical work on popular film and television.

Sparking meaningful interaction between environmental humanities and screen studies in the present study (and beyond) means attending to important debates about Black representation, industry diversity, and Whiteness outside the US context, with the hope of cultivating new directions within ecomedia studies. *Anthroposcreens*'s selective focus on Black US and White Norwegian media representation and production also begs the obvious question: what about Black Norwegian media? In recent years, scholars in the social sciences (Hervik 2019), Scandinavian studies (Körber 2021), Africana studies (Miller and Navarro 2019), and literature (Grydehøj 2020; Teutsch 2021) have actively investigated the contemporary operations of Black identity and color-blind racism in Nordic countries, while within the scholarly field of film and media studies and in the film and television industry, these issues are only beginning to attract attention and promise a rich area for future research. While sociohistorical contexts in the Nordic countries differ both from those of the United States and from one another, much productive ongoing work in the region around topics such as migration, Indigeneity, Whiteness, and nationalism beckons scholars from both film and media studies and the environmental humanities with exciting prospects for concepts that might travel across disciplines.

Meshing approaches from environmental humanities, Black studies, Nordic and Scandinavian studies, critical theories of Whiteness, and film and television studies, *Anthroposcreens* constructs a cultural studies framework to illuminate the intersections of a whole set of "politics," especially climate, racial, and geopolitics. This short Element initiates such interdisciplinary work, bringing into conversation and confrontation key concepts and case studies to open new prospects for combining these important theoretical projects. Examining Black popular media through the Anthropocene lenses of the Plantationocene in *Queen Sugar* and the resource curse in *Black Panther*, Section 2 creates a method for discerning a Black climate unconscious without losing sight of political and aesthetic investments at stake in both Black media studies and in environmental humanities. Tracing the traveling concept of "weathering" in Black studies and environmental humanities, Section 3's juxtaposition of the Black American–centered film *Fast Color* and the White Norwegian fantasy series *Ragnarok* analyzes the next generation of cli-fi and its young heroes, equipped with weather-altering powers. Extending its look into the Norwegian context, *Anthroposcreens* joins the growing inquiry among social scientists into racialization in the Nordic countries through its interrogation of absences and silences in the television series *State of Happiness* and *Occupied*, both in terms of the unmarked dominance of Whiteness and the evasion of petroguilt. These case studies collectively indicate additional directions for future research, and I hope they inspire work on areas that didn't find their way into this study, from disabled, queer, Indigenous and other national or regional contexts, for example. I look forward to the promising future research already underway in the burgeoning field of game studies. And of course, I am already hatching my next plan.

References

Acker, A. (2020). A different story in the Anthropocene: Brazil's post-colonial quest for oil (1930–1975). *Past & Present* **249**(1), 167–211.

Ahmed, S. (2017). *Living a Feminist Life*. Durham, NC: Duke University Press.

Albrecht, G, Gina-Maree Sartore, Linda Connor et al. (2007). Solastalgia: The distress caused by environmental change. *Australasian Psychiatry* **15**(1-suppl), S95–S98.

Andreeva, N. and Petski, D. (2019). *Fast Color* series adaptation in works at Amazon by Viola Davis and Julius Tennon's JuVee Productions. *Deadline*, 30 July. https://deadline.com/2019/07/fast-color-series-adaptation-amazon-viola-davis-julius-tennons-juvee-productions-1202656971/.

Ang, I. (2013). *Watching Dallas: Soap Opera and the Melodramatic Imagination*. London: Routledge.

Appiah, K. A. (2020). The case for capitalizing the "B" in Black. *Atlantic*, June 18. www.theatlantic.com/ideas/archive/2020/06/time-to-capitalize-blackand-white/613159/.

Baden, D. (2018). Environmental storytelling can help spread big ideas for saving the planet. *The Conversation*, 12 August. http://theconversation.com/environmental-storytelling-can-help-spread-big-ideas-for-saving-the-planet-107621.

Bal, M. (2002). *Travelling Concepts in the Humanities: A Rough Guide*. Toronto: University of Toronto Press.

Bartosch, R. (2019). The energy of stories: Postcolonialism, the petroleum unconscious, and the crude side of cultural ecology. *Resilience: A Journal of the Environmental Humanities* **6**(2–3), 116–135.

Bastiaans, A. (2008). Detecting difference in *Devil in a Blue Dress*: The mulatta figure, noir, and the cinematic reification of race. In C. Fojas and M. C. Beltrán, eds., *Mixed Race Hollywood*. New York: New York University Press, pp. 223–247.

Bender, B. (2002). Time and landscape. *Current Anthropology* **43**(S4), S103–S112.

Bennett, M. (2018). What *Black Panther* could mean for the Afrofuturism movement. *Slate*, February 20. https://slate.com/technology/2018/02/what-black-panther-could-mean-for-the-afrofuturism-movement.html.

Bevanger, L. (2020). Norway's richest are richer than we thought. *Nordic Labour Journal*, September 29. www.nordiclabourjournal.org/nyheter/news-2020/article.2020-09-29.4934496755.

References

Bould, M. (2021). *The Anthropocene Unconscious: Climate Catastrophe in Contemporary Culture*. London: Verso.

Brown, J. (2013). *Beasts of the Southern Wild*: The romance of precarity II. *Social Text Online*, September 27. https://socialtextjournal.org/beasts-of-the-southern-wild-the-romance-of-precarity-ii/.

Brownstein, R. (2021). The unbearable summer. *Atlantic*, August 26. www.theatlantic.com/politics/archive/2021/08/summer-2021-climate-change-records/619887/.

Buell, L. (2009). *Writing for an Endangered World*. Cambridge, MA: Harvard University Press.

Carrington, A. M. (2016). *Speculative Blackness: The Future of Race in Science Fiction*. Minneapolis: University of Minnesota Press.

Cartier, N. (2014). Black women on-screen as future texts: A new look at black pop culture representations. *Cinema Journal* **53**(4), 150–157.

Cleary, P. (2016). *Trillion Dollar Baby*. Melbourne: Black.

Connolly, N. D. B. (2018). How *Black Panther* taps into 500 years of history. *Hollywood Reporter*, February 16. www.hollywoodreporter.com/movies/movie-news/black-panther-taps-500-years-history-1085334/.

Cubitt, S. (2005). *EcoMedia*. Amsterdam: Rodopi.

Daggett, C. (2018). Petro-masculinity: Fossil fuels and authoritarian desire. *Millennium: Journal of International Studies* **47**(1), 25–44.

Davis, A. Y. (1998). *Blues Legacies and Black Feminism : Gertrude 'Ma' Rainey, Bessie Smith, and Billie Holiday*. New York: Pantheon Books.

Davis, J. Alex A. Moulton, Levi Van Sant, and Brian Williams. (2019). Anthropocene, Capitalocene, . . . Plantationocene?: A manifesto for ecological justice in an age of global crises. *Geography Compass* **13**(5), e12438.

DeLoughrey, E. (2019). *Allegories of the Anthropocene*. Durham, NC: Duke University Press.

Dery, M. (1994). Black to the future: Interviews with Samuel R. Delany, Greg Tate, and Tricia Rose. In Dery, M., ed., *Flame Wars: The Discourse of Cyberculture*. Durham, NC: Duke University Press, pp. 179–222.

Dowell, B. (2020). *State of Happiness* – the Scandi *Mad Men*? *The Times*, May 7. www.thetimes.co.uk/article/state-of-happiness-the-scandi-mad-men-qsk5cxnss.

Drake, S. C. and Henderson, D. K., eds. (2020). *Are You Entertained? Black Popular Culture in the Twenty-First Century*. Durham, NC: Duke University Press.

Dyer, R. (1997). *White*. New York: Routledge.

Elster, K. (2021). MDG, Rødt og SV foreslår å stoppe all oljeleting på norsk sokkel. *NRK*, October 11. www.nrk.no/norge/mdg_-rodt-og-sv-foreslar-a-stoppe-all-oljeleting-pa-norsk-sokkel-1.15685974.

Fekadu, M. (2021). The sweet rise of *Queen Sugar* director Cierra Glaude. *AP*, February 16. https://apnews.com/article/cierra-glaude-queen-sugar-e55d44f2d3bbab2536d450f8359904ce.

Ferguson, E. (2020). The week in TV. *Guardian*, May 17. www.theguardian .com/tv-and-radio/2020/may/17/hospital-coronavirus-special-review-i-know-this-much-is-true-dave-state-of-happiness-van-der-valk-code-404.

Furuseth, S., Gjelsvik, A., Gürata, A., et al. (2020). Climate change in literature, television, and film from Norway. *Ecozon@: European Journal of Literature, Culture and Environment* **11**(2), 8–16.

Gardner, C. (2019). *Fast Color* filmmaker slams Hollywood's "lip service" to diversity, inclusion. *Hollywood Reporter*, May 9. www.hollywoodreporter .com/news/general-news/fast-color-filmmaker-slams-hollywoods-lip-ser vice-diversity-inclusion-1208479/.

Gates, R. (2017). The last shall be first: Aesthetics and politics in Black film and media. *Film Quarterly* **71**(2), 38–45.

Gates, R. J. and Gillespie, M. B. (2019). Reclaiming Black film and media studies. *Film Quarterly* **72**(3), 13–15.

Gergan, M., Smith, S., and Vasudevan, P. (2020). Earth beyond repair: Race and apocalypse in collective imagination. *Environment and Planning D: Society and Space* **38**(1), 91–110.

Gillespie, M. B. (2016). *Film Blackness: American Cinema and the Idea of Black Film*. Durham, NC: Duke University Press.

Gilroy, P. (1995). *The Black Atlantic: Modernity and Double-Consciousness*. Cambridge, MA: Harvard University Press.

Grusin, R. (2010). *Premediation: Affect and Mediality After 9/11*. London: Palgrave.

Grydehøj, A. (2020). New Scandinavians, new narratives. In A. Lindskog and J. Stougaard-Nielsen, eds., *Introduction to Nordic Cultures*. London: University College London, pp. 146–161.

Gurr, B. (2015). Introduction: After the world ends, again. In B. Gurr, ed., *Race, Gender, and Sexuality in Post-Apocalyptic TV and Film*. London: Palgrave, pp. 1–13.

Hall, S. (1993). What is this "Black" in Black popular culture? *Social Justice* **20** (1–2), 104–114.

Hall, S. (2016). Cultural studies 1983: A theoretical history. In J. D. Slack and L. Grossberg, eds., *Stuart Hall, Selected Writings*. Durham, NC: Duke University Press, pp. 25–53.

Haraway, D. (2015). Anthropocene, Capitalocene, Plantationocene, Chthulucene: Making kin. *Environmental Humanities* **6**(1), 159–165.

Hedden, A. (2021). The desert dries up: New Mexico's water analysis predicts worsening climate change impacts. *Carlsbad Current-Argus*, October 1. www.currentargus.com/story/news/local/2021/10/01/new-mexicos-water-analysis-predicts-worsening-climate-change-impacts/5904992001/.

Hervik, P., ed. (2019). *Racialization, Racism, and Anti-Racism in the Nordic Countries*. Cham: Springer.

Hopewell, J. (2016). Producers Gray and Hummelvoll talk political thriller *Occupied*. *Variety*, February 3. http://variety.com/2016/film/global/gote borg-gray-hummelvoll-political-thriller-occupied-1201695700/.

Horn, E. and Bergthaller, H. (2020). *The Anthropocene: Key Issues for the Humanities*. New York: Routledge.

Huber, M. T. (2013). *Lifeblood: Oil, Freedom, and the Forces of Capital*. Minneapolis: University of Minnesota Press.

Hughes, D. M. (2017). *Energy Without Conscience*. Durham, NC: Duke University Press.

IPCC. (2021). Climate change widespread, rapid, and intensifying. Intergovernmental Panel on Climate Change (blog post). www.ipcc.ch/2021/08/09/ar6-wg1-20210809-pr/.

Ivakhiv, A. (2008). Stirring the geopolitical unconscious: Towards a Jamesonian ecocriticism. *New Formations* **64**, 98–110.

Iversen, G. and Sørenssen, B. (1996). Okkupasjons-dramaene. In H. F. Dahl, J. Gripsrud, G. Iversen, K. Skretting, and B. Sørenssen, *Kinoens Mørke, Fjernsynets Lys: Levende Bilder i Norge Gjennom Hundre År*. Oslo: Gyldendal Norsk Forlag, pp. 191–192.

Jacobs, L. (2014). Sonja Henie's ice age. *Vanity Fair*, 11 February. www .vanityfair.com/hollywood/2014/02/sonja-henie-ice-skating-queen.

Jacobsen, U.C. (2018). Does subtitled television drama brand the nation? Danish television drama and its language(s) in Japan. *European Journal of Cultural Studies* **21**(5), 614–630.

Jameson, F. (1981). *The Political Unconscious: Narrative as a Socially Symbolic Act*. Ithaca, NY: Cornell University Press.

Johnson, J. (2017). Best part of Congressional Black Caucus Week? Exclusive footage of Marvel's *Black Panther*. *The Root*, 25 September. www.theroot .com/best-part-of-congressional-black-caucus-week-exclusive-1818710112.

Jørgensen, F. A. (2015). Why look at cabin porn? *Public Culture* **27**(3), 557–578.

Kääpä, P. (2014). *Ecology and Contemporary Nordic Cinemas: From Nation-Building to Ecocosmopolitanism*. New York: Bloomsbury.

Kaplan, E. A. (2016). *Climate Trauma: Foreseeing the Future in Dystopian Film and Fiction*. New Brunswick, NJ: Rutgers University Press.

Keller, J. (2021). "This Is Oil Country": Mediated transnational girlhood, Greta Thunberg, and patriarchal petrocultures. *Feminist Media Studies* **21**(4), 682–686.

Klein, N. (2008). *The Shock Doctrine: The Rise of Disaster Capitalism*. New York: Picador.

Körber, L.-A. (2021). Exceptionalisms and entanglements: Legacies and memories of Scandinavian colonial history. In T. Jelsbak, J. Bjerring-Hansen, and A. E. Mrozewicz, eds., *Scandinavian Exceptionalisms: Culture, Society, Discourse*. Berlin: Humboldt Universität, pp. 183–204.

Leikam, S. and Leyda, J. (2017). Cli-fi in American studies: A research bibliography. *American Studies Journal* 62. www.asjournal.org/62-2017/cli-fi-american-studies-research-bibliography/.

LeMenager, S. (2014). *Living Oil: Petroleum Culture in the American Century*. New York: Oxford University Press.

Leyda, J. (2016a). *American Mobilities: Geographies of Class, Race, and Gender in US Culture*. Bielefeld: transcript.

Leyda, J. (2016b). The cultural affordances of cli-fi. In *The Dystopian Impulse of Contemporary Cli-Fi*. Potsdam: Institute for Advanced Sustainability Studies. www.iass-potsdam.de/en/output/publications/2016/dystopian-impulse-contemporary-cli-fi-lessons-and-questions-joint-workshop.

Leyda, J. (2018). Petropolitics, cli-fi and *Occupied*. *Journal of Scandinavian Cinema* **8**(2), 83–101.

Leyda, J. (2020). Vekk med gravalvoret! Om humor og ironi i cli-fi. Trans. Ingrid Rommetveit. *Z filmtidsskrift* **151**(2), 68–75.

Leyda, J. (2021). Post-air-conditioning futures and the climate unconscious. *Screen* **62**(1), 100–106.

Leyda, J. and Loock, K. (2022). Climate fiction, dystopias, and human futures. (Video essay). https://vimeo.com/676546312/f8aae10cc3.

Leyda, J. and Negra, D. (2015). Introduction. In J. Leyda and D. Negra, eds., *Extreme Weather and Global Media*. New York: Routledge, pp. 1–28.

Leyda, J. and Negra, D. (2021). Television in/of the banal Anthropocene: Introduction. *Screen* **62**(1), 78–82.

Libell, H. P. and Porter, C. (2018). From Norway to Haiti, Trump's comments stir fresh outrage. *New York Times*, 11 January. www.nytimes.com/2018/01/11/world/trump-countries-haiti-africa.html

Lundström, C. and Teitelbaum, B. R. (2017). Nordic Whiteness: An introduction. *Scandinavian Studies* **89**(2), 151–158.

Malm, A. and Zetkin Collective. (2021). *White Skin, Black Fuel: On the Danger of Fossil Fascism.* London: Verso.

Massood, P. J. (2003). *Black City Cinema: African American Urban Experiences in Film.* Philadelphia, PA: Temple University Press.

Mentz, S. (2019). *Break Up the Anthropocene.* Minneapolis: University of Minnesota Press.

Miller, M. L. and Navarro, T. (2019). Black imaginaries, Scandinavian diasporas. *Barnard College News*, 1 March. https://barnard.edu/news/black-imaginaries-scandinavian-diasporas.

Mirzoeff, N. (2014). Visualizing the Anthropocene. *Public Culture* **26**(2), 213–232.

Morley, D. (2019). General introduction: A life in essays. In S. Hall, *Essential Essays, Volume 1: Foundations of Cultural Studies*, ed. D. Morley. Durham, NC: Duke University Press.

Moynihan, D. P. (1965). *The Moynihan Report: The Negro Family: The Case for National Action.* Cosimo Reports. Washington, DC: The Department of Labor.

Mrozewicz, A. E. (2020). The landscapes of eco-noir: Reimagining Norwegian eco-exceptionalism in *Occupied*. *Nordicom Review* **41**(s1), 85–105.

Muller Myrdahl, E. (2014). Recuperating whiteness in the injured nation: Norwegian identity in the response to 22 July. *Social Identities* **20**(6), 486–500.

Næss, E. M. (2020). Jotner. *Store norske leksikon*. http://snl.no/jotner.

Narine, A. ed. (2014). *Eco-Trauma Cinema.* New York: Routledge.

Negra, D. (2001). *Off-White Hollywood: American Culture and Ethnic Female Stardom.* New York: Routledge.

Neimanis, A. and Hamilton, J. M. (2018). Weathering. *Feminist Review* **118**(1), 80–84.

Nesbø, J. (2014). Jo Nesbø on *The Redbreast. Guardian*, 2 May. www.theguardian.com/books/2014/may/02/jo-nesbo-the-redbreast-guardian-book-club.

Newkirk, II, V. R. (2018). The provocation and power of *Black Panther. Atlantic*, 14 February. www.theatlantic.com/entertainment/archive/2018/02/the-provocation-and-power-of-black-panther/553226/.

Nilsen, M.S. (2020). *Ragnarok*: Norrønt nonsens. *VG* 30 January. www.vg.no/i/EWggR2.

Nixon, R. (2011). *Slow Violence and the Environmentalism of the Poor.* Cambridge, MA: Harvard University Press.

Norgaard, K. M. (2011). *Living in Denial: Climate Change, Emotions, and Everyday Life.* Cambridge, MA: MIT Press.

Økland, A. (2018). Norge trenger en serie som *Lykkeland. Dagbladet*, November 3. www.dagbladet.no/kultur/norge-trenger-en-serie-som-lykkeland/70394964.

Okuyade, O. (2011). Rethinking militancy and environmental justice: The politics of oil and violence in Nigerian popular music. *Africa Today* **58**(1), 78–101.

Onyebuchi, T. (2018). Homecoming: How Afrofuturism bridges the past and the present. *Tor.com*, February 27. www.tor.com/2018/02/27/homecoming-how-afrofuturism-bridges-the-past-and-the-present/.

Oppermann, S. and Iovino, S. (2017). Introduction: The environmental humanities and the challenge of the Anthropocene. In S. Oppermann and S. Iovino, eds., *Environmental Humanities: Voices from the Anthropocene*. London: Rowman & Littlefield.

Oxfeldt, E. (2016). *Skandinaviske fortellinger om skyld og privilegier i en globaliseringstid*. Oslo: Universitetsforlaget.

Painter, N. I. (2020). Why "White" should be capitalized, too. *Washington Post*, July 22. www.washingtonpost.com/opinions/2020/07/22/why-white-should-be-capitalized/.

Pham, A. (2018). Bølstad and Hørsdal on how oil created happiness in Norway. *Nordisk Film og TV Fond*, April 8. www.nordiskfilmogtvfond.com/news/interview/bolstad-and-horsdal-on-how-oil-created-a-state-of-happiness-in-norway.

Pick, A. and G. Narraway, eds. (2013). *Screening Nature: Cinema beyond the Human*. New York: Berghahn Books.

Pierrot, B. and Seymour, N. (2020). Contemporary cli-fi and Indigenous futurisms. *Departures in Critical Qualitative Research* **9**(4), 92–113.

Pitcher, B. (2014). *Consuming Race*. New York: Routledge.

Polan, D. (2013). Maddening times: *Mad Men* in its history. In L. M. E. Goodlad, L. Kaganovsky, and R. A. Rushing, eds., *Mad Men, Mad World: Sex, Politics, Style, and the 1960s*. Durham, NC: Duke University Press, pp. 35–52.

Ramadan, L., Ngu, A., and Miller, M. (2021). The smoke comes every year: Sugar companies say the air is safe. *ProPublica*, July 8. https://projects.propublica.org/black-snow/.

Rastas, A. (2019). The emergence of race as a social category in northern Europe. In P. Essed, K. Farquharson, K. Pillay, E. J. White, eds., *Relating Worlds of Racism*. Cham: Springer, pp. 357–381.

Ray, S. J. (2020). *A Field Guide to Climate Anxiety*. Berkeley: University of California Press.

Ray, S. J. (2021). Climate anxiety is an overwhelmingly white phenomenon. *Scientific American*, May 6. www.scientificamerican.com/article/the-unbearable-whiteness-of-climate-anxiety/.

Rees, E. (2016). Privilege, innocence, and "petro-guilt" in Maria Sødahl's *Limbo. Scandinavian Studies* **88**(1), 42–59.

Ritson, K. (2019). *The Shifting Sands of the North Sea Lowlands: Literary and Historical Imaginaries*. London: Routledge.

Rodney, W. (1972). *How Europe Underdeveloped Africa*. Baltimore, MD: Black Classic.

Rowat, A. (2020). TV review: *State of Happiness. HeraldScotland*, May 9. www.heraldscotland.com/arts_ents/18432931.tv-review-state-happiness-inside-central-station-word-first-dates-hotel/.

Rugg, L. H. (2017). Displacing crimes against nature: Scandinavian ecocrime fiction. *Scandinavian Studies* **89**(4), 597–615.

Saunders, R. A. (2020). Landscape, geopolitics, and national identity in the Norwegian thrillers *Occupied* and *Nobel*. *Nordicom Review* **41**(s1), 63–83.

Scott, H. P. (2020). Offshore mysteries, narrative infrastructure: Oil, noir, and the world-ocean. *Humanities* **9**(3), 1–15.

Seierstad, Å. (2019). The anatomy of White terror. *New York Times*, March 18. www.nytimes.com/2019/03/18/opinion/new-zealand-tarrant-white-supremacist-terror.html.

Seymour, N. (2013). *Strange Natures: Futurity, Empathy, and the Queer Ecological Imagination*. Urbana: University of Illinois Press.

Seymour, N. (2018). *Bad Environmentalism: Irony and Irreverence in the Ecological Age*. Minneapolis: University of Minnesota Press.

Sharpe, C. (2013). *Beasts of the Southern Wild*: The romance of precarity I. *Social Text Online*. https://socialtextjournal.org/beasts-of-the-southern-wild-the-romance-of-precarity-i/.

Sharpe, C. (2016). *In the Wake: On Blackness and Being*. Durham, NC: Duke University Press.

Shaviro, S. (2016). Post-cinematic affect. In S. Denson and J. Leyda, eds., *Post-Cinema: Theorizing 21st-Century Film*. Falmer: Reframe.

Smith-Shomade, B. E., Gates, R., and Petty, M. J. (2014). Introduction: When and where we enter. *Cinema Journal* **53**(4), 121–127.

Stewart, J. (2017). Resource curse. In I. Szeman, J. Wenzel, and P. Yaeger, eds., *Fueling Culture: 101 Words for Energy and Environment*. New York: Fordham University Press, pp. 285–288.

Stougaard-Nielsen, J. (2016). Nordic noir in the UK: The allure of accessible difference. *Journal of Aesthetics & Culture* **8**(1), n.p.

Stratigakos, D. (2020). *Hitler's Northern Utopia: Building the New Order in Occupied Norway*. Princeton, NJ: Princeton University Press.

Streeby, S. (2017). *Imagining the Future of Climate Change: World-Making through Science Fiction and Activism*. Berkeley: University of California Press.

Sulimma, M. (2021). *Gender and Seriality: Practices and Politics of Contemporary US Television*. Edinburgh: University of Edinburgh Press.

Svoboda, M. (2016). Cli-fi on the screen(s): patterns in the representations of climate change in fictional films. *WIREs Climate Change*, **7**(1), 43–64. DOI: https://doi.org/10.1002/wcc.381.

Swanson, H. A. (2017). The banality of the Anthropocene. *Society for Cultural Anthropology*, February 22. https://culanth.org/fieldsights/the-banality-of-the-anthropocene.

Szeman, I. (2017). On the politics of extraction. *Cultural Studies* **31**(2–3): 440–447.

Teutsch, M. (2021). Blackness, Norwegian identity, and nationality. *Black Perspectives*, July 23. www.aaihs.org/blackness-norwegian-identity-and-nationality/.

Thomas, C. (2018). "Black" comics as a cultural archive of Black life in America. *Feminist Media Histories* **4**(3), 49–95.

Thorvik, H. B. (2020). Like dårlig som det høres ut. *Dagbladet*, January 28. www.dagbladet.no/kultur/like-darlig-som-det-hores-ut/72072193.

Thue, L. (2008). Norway: A resource-based and democratic capitalism. In S. Fellman, M. Iversen, H. Sjögren, and L. Thue, eds., *Creating Nordic Capitalism: The Development of a Competitive Periphery*. London: Palgrave.

Trenka, S. (2014). Appreciation, appropriation, assimilation: *Stormy Weather* and the Hollywood history of Black dance. In M. B. Borelli, ed., *Oxford Handbook of Dance and the Popular Screen*. London: Oxford University Press, pp. 98–112.

Turner, G. (2006). *Film as Social Practice*. 4th ed. London: Routledge.

Tuskegee Study – Timeline – CDC (2020). www.cdc.gov/tuskegee/timeline .htm.

Ugwu, R. (2019). They set us up to fail: Black directors of the '90s speak out. *New York Times*, July 3. www.nytimes.com/2019/07/03/movies/black-directors-1990s.html.

Ummelas, O. (2021). Norway's Labor, Center agree to form pro-oil minority coalition. *Bloomberg.com*, October 8. www.bloomberg.com/news/articles/2021-10-08/norway-s-labor-center-agree-to-form-pro-oil-minority-coalition.

Van Dam, A. (2018). Norway was once the kind of country Trump might've spit on: Now its people don't even want to come here. *Washington Post*, January 12. www.washingtonpost.com/news/wonk/wp/2018/01/12/trump-wants-more-immigrants-from-norway-theres-a-reason-they-arent-coming/.

Vik, S. M. (2017). Petro-images of the Arctic and Statoil's visual imaginary. In L.-A. Körber, S. MacKenzie, and A. Westerståhl Stenport, eds., *Arctic Environmental Modernities*. Cham: Springer, pp. 43–58.

Vogel, S. (2008). Performing "Stormy Weather": Ethel Waters, Lena Horne, and Katherine Dunham. *South Central Review* **25**(1), 93–113.

Waade, A. M. (2017). Melancholy in Nordic noir: Characters, landscapes, light, and music. *Critical Studies in Television* **12**(4), 380–94.

Wallace, C. (2018). Why "Black Panther" is a defining moment for Black America. *New York Times*, February 12. www.nytimes.com/2018/02/12/magazine/why-black-panther-is-a-defining-moment-for-black-america.html.

Wallace, M. (1978). *Black Macho and the Myth of the Superwoman*. London: Verso.

Warner, K. J. (2017). In the time of plastic representation. *Film Quarterly* **71**(2), 32–37.

Warner, K. J. (2021). Blue skies again: Streamers and the impossible promise of diversity. *Los Angeles Review of Books*, June 24. https://lareviewofbooks.org/article/blue-skies-again-streamers-and-the-impossible-promise-of-diversity/.

Weik von Mossner, A., ed. (2014). *Moving environments: Affect, emotion, ecology, and film*. Waterloo, ON: Wilfrid Laurier University Press.

Wearden, G. (2023). "Ridiculous": Greta Thunberg blasts decision to let UAE oil boss chair climate talks. *The Guardian*, January 19.

Wenzel, J. (2017). Introduction: Fueling culture. In I. Szeman, J. Wenzel, and P. Yaeger, eds., *Fueling Culture: 101 Words for Energy and Environment*. New York: Fordham University Press.

Whyte, K. P. (2017). Our ancestors' dystopia now: Indigenous conservation and the Anthropocene. In U. K. Heise, J. Christensen, and M. Niemann, eds., *Routledge Companion to the Environmental Humanities*. London: Routledge, pp. 206–215.

Wilkinson, A. (2018). *Black Panther* crushed overseas sales projections. Can we stop saying Black films don't travel? *Vox*, February 20. www.vox.com/culture/2018/2/20/17029156/black-panther-international-overseas-box-office-black-films-hidden-figures-proud-mary.

Williams, J. (2018). Wakanda shakes the world. *Foreign Policy*, April 1. https://foreignpolicy.com/2018/04/01/wakanda-shakes-the-world/.

Williams, S. (2019). *Queen Sugar*'s women directors: Nourishing complex images. *Feminist Media Studies* **19**(7), 1043–1046.

Willoquet-Maricondi, P., ed. (2010). *Framing the World: Explorations in Ecocriticism and Film*. Charlottesville: University of Virginia Press.

Wilson, J. (2016). The meaning of #BlackGirlMagic, and how you can get some of it. *HuffPost*, January 12. www.huffpost.com/entry/what-is-black-girl-magic-video_n_5694dad4e4b086bc1cd517f4.

Wilson, S., Carlson, A., and Szeman, I., eds. (2017). *Petrocultures: Oil, Politics, Culture*. Montreal: McGill-Queen's University Press.

Witoszek, N. and Midttun, A. eds. (2018). *Sustainable Modernity: The Nordic Model and Beyond*. London: Routledge.

Womack, Y. L. (2013). *Afrofuturism: The World of Black Sci-Fi and Fantasy Culture*. Chicago: Chicago Review Press.

Worden, D. (2012). Fossil-fuel futurity: Oil in *Giant*. *Journal of American Studies* **46**(2), 441–460.

Wu, J., Snell, G., and Samji, H. (2020). Climate anxiety in young people: A call to action. *The Lancet Planetary Health* **4**(10), e435–e436.

Yaeger, P. (2011). Editor's Column: Literature in the ages of wood, tallow, coal, whale oil, gasoline, atomic power, and other energy sources. *PMLA* **126**(2), 305–326.

Yates, M. (2018). Whiteness, masculinity, and environmental nostalgia in *Soylent Green* and *WALL-E*, in B. Barclay and C. Tidwell, eds., *Gender and Environment in Science Fiction*. London: Rowman & Littlefield, pp. 167–184.

Yusoff, K. (2018). *A Billion Black Anthropocenes or None*. Minneapolis: University of Minnesota Press.

Zamalin, A. (2019). *Black Utopia: The History of an Idea from Black Nationalism to Afrofuturism*. New York: Columbia University Press.

Zhang, S. (2018). The surgeon who experimented on slaves. *Atlantic*, April 18. www.theatlantic.com/health/archive/2018/04/j-marion-sims/558248/.

Zylinska, J. (2018). *The End of Man: A Feminist Counterapocalypse*. Minneapolis: University of Minnesota Press.

Acknowledgments

Written during the pandemic and revised while disabled by long COVID, this Element is both a miracle and a compromise. I dedicate it in solidarity to all my fellow scholars going through this, no matter how much or how little work we did.

Massive thanks to friends and colleagues on endless video chats acting as cheering section, sob sisters, and comrades in the struggle, especially weekly online *skrivepress* with Nina Lager Vestberg, Margrethe Stang, Ingrid Lunnan Nødseth, Ilona Hongisto, and Anne Marit Myrstad. Sissel Furuseth's Collaboratory on Critical Petroaesthetics at the Oslo School of Environmental Humanities has been inspiring, as have all my collaborations with Katie Ritson. The RCC "COVID-cohort" provided excellent feedback on a draft of Section 4, especially Johanna Conterio, Antoine Acker, and Stephen Halsey. It was a joy to work with so many world-class scholars there, even after lockdown closed the Glühwein kiosks. Thanks to Kathleen Loock, Imre Szeman, Jennifer Wenzel, Diane Negra, Arthur Mason, Alexander Klose, Benjamin Steininger, Anne Marit Waade, Irina Souch, Robert Saunders, Henrik Bødker, Marion Grau, Thomas Patrick Pringle, and Christopher Shore for comments at various stages. For supportive comments, emojis, and camaraderie, I will always be indebted to Nina Lager Vestberg, Maria Sulimma, and Nicole Seymour.

Laura Portwood-Stacer's brilliant Book Proposal Accelerator helped me realize I wasn't ready to take on a full-length monograph, but that I did have something I wanted to write. Spot-on developmental editing from Micha Rahder at Ideas on Fire was exactly what I needed, when I needed it. I am exceptionally privileged to work in a department that prioritizes and pays for author support services like these, and for the additional fees to make this text open access. Funded stays at the Freie Universität Berlin, the Institute for Advanced Sustainability Studies at Potsdam, and the Rachel Carson Center for Environment and Society also freed me for extended periods of research.

Sections of this Element grew out of teaching and talks at the Lübeck Film Studies Colloquium, IASS Potsdam, Kunsthall Trondheim, the University of Vienna, the University of Lund, the Freie Universität Berlin, the Arctic University of Norway in Tromsø, the University of Agder, Aarhus University, the 2018 Literature/Film Adaptation conference in New Orleans, the 2018 Norwegian Media Studies Association conference in Bodø, the 2019 NordMedia conference in Malmø, the 2019 Society for Cinema and Media Studies conference in Seattle, and the 2019 Oslo Film Seminar of the Norwegian Federation of Film Societies.

Cambridge Elements

Environmental Humanities

Louise Westling
University of Oregon

Louise Westling is an American scholar of literature and environmental humanities who was a founding member of the Association for the Study of Literature and Environment and its President in 1998. She has been active in the international movement for environmental cultural studies, teaching and writing on landscape imagery in literature, critical animal studies, biosemiotics, phenomenology, and deep history.

Serenella Iovino
University of North Carolina at Chapel Hill

Serenella Iovino is Professor of Italian Studies and Environmental Humanities at the University of North Carolina at Chapel Hill. She has written on a wide range of topics, including environmental ethics and ecocritical theory, bioregionalism and landscape studies, ecofeminism and posthumanism, comparative literature, eco-art, and the Anthropocene.

Timo Maran
University of Tartu

Timo Maran is an Estonian semiotician and poet. Maran is Professor of Ecosemiotics and Environmental Humanities and Head of the Department of Semiotics at the University of Tartu. His research interests are semiotic relations of nature and culture, Estonian nature writing, zoosemiotics and species conservation, and semiotics of biological mimicry.

About the Series

The environmental humanities is a new transdisciplinary complex of approaches to the embeddedness of human life and culture in all the dynamics that characterize the life of the planet. These approaches reexamine our species' history in light of the intensifying awareness of drastic climate change and ongoing mass extinction. To engage this reality, Cambridge Elements in Environmental Humanities builds on the idea of a more hybrid and participatory mode of research and debate, connecting critical and creative fields.

Cambridge Elements ≡

Environmental Humanities

Elements in the Series

A full series listing is available at: www.cambridge.org/EIEH

Printed in the United States
by Baker & Taylor Publisher Services